ELEVEN HOLY DISCOURSES OF PROTECTION

Mahā Paritta Pāḷi

ELEVEN HOLY DISCOURSES OF PROTECTION

Mahā Paritta Pāḷi

Transliterated and
Translated from the Burmese Pāḷi Scriptures
(The Sixth Buddhist Council Version)
into English

by

Sao Htun Hmat Win
M.A; A.M; S.R.F. (Harvard)
Director Of Research and Scriptures

Edited by

Kaba-Aye U Chit Tin

MPA Pariyatti Editions
an imprint of
Pariyatti Publishing
www.pariyatti.org

First printed in 1981
First Pariyatti Edition 2024

ISBN: 978-1-68172-690-8 (print)
ISBN: 978-1-68172-691-5 (PDF)
ISBN: 978-1-68172-692-2 (ePub)
ISBN: 978-1-68172-693-9 (Mobi)
Library of Congress Control Number: 2024936811

THE AUTHOR

The nativity of Sao Htun Hmat Win, the eldest son of U Gaw Yar (a) Sao Sam Hlaing and Nang Htay Htay was celebrated at Fort Stedman in Mong Hsauk Township of Yawnghwe State in the Shan Hills, on the 12th of August 1925.

He got through his elementary, secondary and higher education in Mong Hsawk, Yawnghwe, and Taunggyi American Boys' High School successively, receiving outstanding awardments of Federation Scholarship. In 1942 he received the Diploma in Teaching of Japanese Language with first class honors.

Sao Htun Hmat Win was awarded the Rangoon University Collegiate Scholarship and the President's Prize of Distinction in the Matriculation Examination in 1947.

Fully ordained as a monk with an epithet of Rev: Vaṇṇadhajasīri, he passed the Lower, the Middle, and the Higher monastic examinations in Buddhist canonical scriptures. He also won first prizes in Literary Contests sponsored by the National Fine Arts and University Burmese Association (1949–50).

Sao Htun Hmat Win graduated from Rangoon University with degrees of B.A. Hons: in 1952, M.A. in 1954, and was granted the Special Research Scholar Awardment in 1957 at the International Institute for Advanced Buddhistic Studies.

Nominated by the Government, he was sent abroad to the United States of America and had successfully gone through his master's degree in the History and Philosophy of Religion at Harvard Graduate School of Arts and Sciences. He was also enrolled in the Ph.D. Class as a Senior Research Fellow at the Harvard Divinity School in the Comparative Study of World Religions Program (1959–62).

In 1962 he returned home, to serve at the International Institute for Advanced Buddhistic Studies as Head of the Research Department and eventually as the Director of Research in the Ministry of Religious Affairs.

In 1968 he gained the National Literary Award for his masterpiece, "Elements of Research Methods". Having enlisted as a pioneer member of the Writers and Journalists Organisation, he had devoted himself in research works for decades and contributed 27 books to the world of knowledge. He reads various languages, such as Shan, Burmese, English, Japanese, German, Pāḷi, Sanskrit, French, and Tibetan to engender his intensive research exploration.

Well-known in the country for his piety and devotion in religion, this scholar, Sao Htun Hmat Win, at the age of 55, soon after his publications of "The Mudrās in Burmese Buddhist Iconography" and "The Seats, Postures, Vehicles in Burmese Buddhist Iconography with a Historical Sketch of Burmese Buddhist Culture", here again presents another invaluable treatise, "The Eleven Holy Discourses of Protection," or "The Mahā Paritta Suttas" and "Pabbājaniya Kammavācā."

ACKNOWLEDGMENTS

I express my deepest feeling of regard and gratitude to Professor Dr. Elizabeth K. Nottingham who as my affectionate proctor took pains to go through the entire manuscripts with scrupulous care, suggesting improvements, and always favouring me with her wide scholarship and experience. She opened the doors for my further studies abroad and she released all that she could to make my three years stay in U.S.A. profitable. It was through her kind efforts and by virtue of her recommendations that the authority of the Harvard University in New England States gave me special privilege as a Senior Research Fellow to study in the program of PH.D. in the History and Philosophy of Religion.

To Nang Htay Htay of the Harvard Graduate School of Education and also to Dr. Robert Lawson Slator of the Center for the Study of World Religions, Harvard Divinity School, I take the opportunity to offer my sincere thanks and gratitude. Their words of encouragement and affectionate concern for success in my endeavours have been a source of strength and inspiration to me. My feeling of regard and gratitude towards these three people are too deep for words and I cannot do more than merely record here my indebtedness to them.

This treatise owes its publication in this present form to the generosity of Daw Khin Thein Dine (Synthia) who even in the midst of her heavy duties at the Institute of Education, has spared her precious time, to go through my papers and has contributed her wise suggestions to improve my command of English language and she deserves my highest gratitude. I treasure here the ever-affectionate memory of her collaboration and friendship.

Of course, I thank most sincerely the International Institute for Advanced Buddhistic Studies, for without which I would have no privilege to bring about this writing.

Sao Htun Hmat Win
Rangoon, Burma
August, 1980

CONTENTS

The Author v
Acknowledgments vii

Method of Translation 1
Buddhism as Religion 2
Apotropaic Buddhism 4
Eleven Mahā Paritta Suttas 8
Textual Resources 10
Paritta as Bhāvanā Meditation 16
Recite and Work 17

MAHĀ PARITTA PĀḶI
The Text of Great Protection 20
[1] **Maṅgala Sutta**
The Discourse on Auspices 22
[2] **Ratana Sutta**
The Discourse on Precious Jewels 26
[3] **Mettā Sutta**
The Discourse on Lovingkindness 33
[4] **Khandha Sutta**
The Discourse on Protection of the Aggregates 37
[5] **Mora Sutta**
The Discourse on the Peacock's Prayer 40
[6] **Vaṭṭa Sutta**
The Discourse on the Quail's Asseveration 44
[7] **Dhajagga Sutta**
The Discourse on the Crest of Banners 46

[8] **Āṭānāṭiya Sutta**
The Discourse on Āṭānāṭiya 51
[9] **Aṅgulimāla Sutta**
The Act of Truth by Reverend Aṅgulimāla 56
[10] **Bojjhaṅga Sutta**
The Discourse on the Seven Factors of Enlightenment 59
[11] **Pubbaṇha Sutta**
The Discourse on Good Morning 63

MAHĀ PARITTA PĀḶI (Transliteration) 67
Mahā Paritta Pāḷi 69
Maṅgala Sutta 71
Ratana Sutta 73
Mettā Sutta 77
Khandha Sutta 79
Mora Sutta 80
Vaṭṭa Sutta 81
Dhajagga Sutta 82
Āṭānāṭiya Sutta 86
Aṅgulimāla Sutta 89
Bojjhaṅga Sutta 90
Pubbaṇha Sutta 91

Monastic Sanction of Act of Banishment 94
Pabbājaniya Kammavācā 96

METHOD OF TRANSLATION

This is my modest confession. To the best of my ability and confidence in this instance, I am rendering the original version of the book of eleven *Mahā Paritta Suttas* in Burmese Pāḷi into English. The translation has been so attempted that it will be as close to the literal Pāḷi phrases as possible. In order to serve the readers a very faithful and readable rendering, the Pāḷi stanzas have been translated and interpreted in word for word transformative design.

I have also endeavoured sincerely to help the readers to be able to refer to the original Pāḷi text, by indicating the number of the Pāḷi stanza at the head of each translated paragraph. To be in accordance with the standardised Sixth Buddhist Council version of the *Mahā Paritta Pāḷi* text printed in Burma (1956), the total number of stanzas in this book is set at 164.

The English syntax may sometimes be not too clear or exact, but if the readers can grasp the inherent meaning and intrinsic value of the discourses, however vague this work, must be considered satisfactory.

BUDDHISM AS RELIGION

Moreover, to elucidate the unintelligible meaning of some passages in the translation, I have provided a brief historical sketch of each discourse at the beginning of every Sutta. This may serve as the exegetical introduction to each *Paritta Sutta*.

Not being contented with such a technical endeavour, I have committed myself to a research exploration on the religious character of Burmese Buddhism in conjunction with the eleven *Paritta Suttas*.

In this presentation I am not prepared to argue about the salient diversity in the definitions of the term "Buddhism". The readers may already have conceived that Buddhism is all encompassing, wholesome, meaningful, global, and a humanistic social philosophy, though it may sometimes be with reference to the context, philosophical, theological, ethical, psychological, historical, mystical, and *Religious*.

This is a researcher's attempt to consider briefly the religious position of Burmese Buddhism and to reveal the status of *Mahā Parittas* text in Buddhism, being prayers for prosperity and safety of the Buddhists in Burma.

I am quite reluctant to pronounce that Buddhism is a Religion, however, I have to admit that there are many vital religious elements enshrined in this faith, especially in Burmese Buddhism which usually claims to be the Pristine Form of Theravada Buddhist Tradition.

In the daily life of a Burman Buddhist, critically speaking, the outlook is very much religious as in other great world religions. The following statements may reveal how much Burmese Buddhism is religious.

Buddhism is an Ideological System. It is a religion of Explicit Salvation and hence is to be called Nibbanic Buddhism.

Again, it is a religion of Proximate Salvation and therefore can be classified as Kammatic Buddhism.

It may even be typified as a religion of chiliastic Expectations, for imminent and imminent salvation, the enjoyment of a better world as an event which occurs within history, to be known as Esoteric Buddhism.

It is quite obvious that Buddhism has a well-established monastic system too. Its normative structure, social structure, recruitment structure, character structure, and even the status of monkhood in Burmese society can be all treated as the components of a religious institution.

And sometimes Buddhism can be treated as a Ritual System too, being endowed with various rites and rituals, the obvious characteristic of a typical religion.

More specifically, Buddhism has an apotropaic phenomenon, which also indicates it to be a religion of magical protection.

APOTROPAIC BUDDHISM

Of all the above-mentioned religious characteristics of Burmese Buddhism, this article is to discuss the Apotropaic issue, the religious phenomena of Magical protection.

Apotropaion is a technical term derived from Greek, which means any amulet or supposed charm against evil influences.

Apotropaic therefore indicates averting evil of or pertaining to an apotropaion.

Let us presume here, for the benefit of academic discussion, that apotropaic Buddhism is one of the peculiar phases of the faith in Burmese tradition. And the discussion will be encompassed within the boundary of apotropaic approach, even when we deal with the *Mahā Paritta Sutta* discourses.

Apotropaic Buddhism is concerned with important matters in this present existence, illness and death, drought and rain, calamity and tranquility, danger, and security.

It also, assumes that the goals involved here can be attained by specific magical acts which either generate immediate power or invoke the assistance of supernatural forces. For apotropaic Buddhism the religion as a whole (its devotion, ritual, ethics, scripture, and what not) acts as protective measures against the dangers of the present existence. The world (*Loka*) is viewed by Burmans to be dangerous because ghosts, demons, evil spirits, Nats, and other evil souls are existing everywhere; one is constantly and unpredictably in danger of being harmed. Therefore, Buddhism is a refuge against all these dangers. Security is achieved by Buddhistic means. Buddhism prevails as the haven of the

Burmese people. Most of the Burmese Buddhist rituals are apotropaic and they are performed to extricate the believer from a calamity which he is now suffering, or to save the devotee from the danger which is impending. There are causes and occasions of these calamities and dangers.

They are:

1) Natural Kammaic and
2) Supernatural Kammaic resources.

Because of natural Kammaic reasons, ills, hazards, and miserable troubles come into existence. For instance, accidents, imprisonment, sickness, dog bites, snake hits, drought, loss of wealth, defamation and other inevitable quarrels and fights are the resultant issues of natural kammaic resources. Such imminent and critical problems are solved in a variety of ways by Burmans. Medical treatments are given to the sick; agrarian and irrigation systems are improved and materialized to afford protection against famine and drought; legal, social, and political measures are carried out to help those who have breached laws and regulations. Yet these solutions are sometimes ineffective. If these problems cannot be sufficiently coped with, by such naturalistic techniques, Burmese Buddhists customarily resort to rituals of apotropaic Buddhism or Buddhist magical rituals.

Where the dangers and perils are not overcome by naturalistic techniques, then the causes of the incidents are ascribed to supernatural kammaic reasons such as witchcraft, spirits, planetary influence, charms and bad luck.

Astrological influence on the daily life of a Burman is great. The Brahmins (*Poṇṇahs*) are hereditary astrological advisors to the Burmese families. Planetary reflections upon the destiny of the individual and the nation are watched with great interest, whether beneficent or maleficent. Immediate necessary actions must be carried out to avoid in time when signs of unhappy planetary influence are detected.

Good and bad omens are also interpreted seriously by the nation or by the individual, and effective preventions must be carried out promptly. In such events the use of Buddhist sacra or spells for protection against the above-mentioned dangers must be employed. The devout Burman must tell many rounds of rosary beads daily citing the Buddhist sacra.

Building of pagodas, constructing of roads and bridges; setting free fish or any living animal from the hands of fishmongers or butchers, or in the least to support the branches and water the Bodhi trees, must be done to avoid those forthcoming dangers and disasters. Sometimes the Nine Buddhas or the Dakkhiṇasākhā image of the Buddha must be consecrated and honoured by the help of Buddhist monks to avert the predicted calamities.

Very often the yellow robe of the Buddha or of a respectable monk is considered to be endowed with magical power as protection against evil supernatural forces. Hence the ultimate protection for a victim is to be ordained as a Buddhist monk, to be able to don the yellow monastic robe, even if for a temporary period. Such a monk is known as Dullabha Rahan.

Buddhist spells in verbal formula are known as *Gāthā* or *Mantrāh*, the chanting of which is believed to achieve a desired result by generating magical power or by compelling the assistance of superhuman divinities. *Parittas* or *Rakkhaṇas* are originally prayers for prosperity, safety, and the welfare of the Buddhist devotees in Burma, but gradually the *Paritta*

Gāthās become Buddhist spells. *Paritta* is a technical term derived from the root:

tā - (*rakkhati*) to rescue, to protect, to guard; with the prefix

pari - all around (*samantato*), from all directions.

Paritta may therefore be interpreted as Buddhist Protecting Charms or Buddhist *Raksha Mantras*. *Mahā* means great, holy, sacred, auspicious, mighty, abundant. Thus, the great collection of Buddhist spells is generally known as *Mahā Paritta Suttas* in Burma.

ELEVEN MAHĀ PARITTA SUTTAS

Among the categories of spells, the most important one is the collection of eleven *Paritta Suttas*. These *Paritta Suttas* are recited either individually or collectively in unison. Some or all of these *suttas* are recited as part of regular Buddhist devotions, to protect against dangers and calamities, whether they are natural or supernatural. To prevent oncoming unhappy events and to eradicate the hazards which have already happened are two main purposes of recitation on special occasions.

It is worthy to note that each *Paritta Sutta* has a specific function, though any *paritta* can be recited for general protective measure. Thus, for example, *Aṅgulimāla Paritta* must be chanted in case of difficult childbirth; *Khandha Paritta* against snake bites and poisoning; *Vaṭṭa Paritta* to calm down the burning fire; *Mora Paritta* to release oneself from imprisonment; *Bojjhaṅga Paritta* to cure the illness of critical patients, and so on.

Mahā Paritta Suttas become therefore the indispensable element in the security system of the Burmese Buddhist world. Without this core of Burmese ritual, no crisis can be confronted, and almost all problematic crises are solved by them. The Burmese monks are responsible to perform the recitation ritual on behalf of the lay devotees. It is inconceivable for a member of the Burmese Buddhist church to refuse to perform such *paritta* recitation when requested by his devotees.

All eleven *Paritta Suttas* are prescribed in the Traditional Burmese monastic education, and the young scholars, neophytes, novices, and deacons (*Kyaungtha, Pothudaw, Koyin,* and *Upazin*) are trained to memorize them right from the original Pāḷi texts. All of these texts have been translated into Burmese vernacular language and every grown-up Burman is supposed to understand some or all of these suttas when the elder monks recite in Pāḷi on behalf of the householders in the village ceremonies. This religious practice is still in vogue in Burmese Buddhist society.

TEXTUAL RESOURCES

The Burmese Buddhists pay equal respect to these eleven *Mahā Paritta Suttas* as they do to the canonical literature (*Tipiṭaka Pāḷi*). In spite of many later expositions and interpolations in the *Paritta* compilation, by ancient learned sages, all these suttas are essentially based upon the canonical discourses.

1) *Maṅgala Sutta* is based on *Khuddapāṭha* and *Suttanipāta* texts, in *Khuddaka Nikāya.*
2) *Ratana Paritta* is based on *Khuddapāṭha* and *Suttanipāta* texts, in *Khuddaka Nikāya.*
3) *Mettā Paritta* is based on *Khuddapāṭha* and *Suttanipāta* texts, in *Khuddaka Nikāya.*
4) *Khandha Paritta* is based on *Vinaya Piṭaka Cūḷavagga*, *Jātaka*, and *Aṅguttara Nikāya* texts.
5) *Mora Paritta* is based on *Jātaka* text in *Khuddaka Nikāya.*
6) *Vaṭṭa Paritta* is based on *Jātaka* and *Cariyāpiṭaka* texts in *Khuddaka Nikāya.*
7) *Dhajagga Paritta* is based on *Saṃyutta Nikāya, Sakka Saṃyutta* text.
8) *Ātānāṭiya Paritta* is based on *Dīgha Nikāya – Pāthikavagga* text and *Dhammapada* text in *Khuddaka Nikāya.*
9) *Aṅgulimāla Paritta* is based on *Majjhima Nikāya – Majjhimapaṇṇāsa* text.
10) *Bojjhaṅga sutta* is based on *Saṃyutta Nikāya, Mahāvagga Saṃyutta* text.
11) *Pubbaṇha sutta* is based on *Khuddakapāṭha, Suttanipāta* texts in *Khuddaka Nikāya*, and *Aṅguttara Nikāya* texts.

Historical Resources

There are historical evidences that *parittas* have been recited in Burma from the very earliest pre-Pagan times. According to the History of Buddhist Religion (*Sāsanā-vaṃsa*), Elder Sona and Elder Uttara came into Burma, *Suvaṇṇabhūmi*, as Buddhist missionaries, or at least as *Dharma-mahāmantras* despatched by King Asoka to propagate the Teachings of the Buddha. And they chanted Brahmajāla Sutta as *paritta* to protect the children of the country from the demons (*Pisācas*) who used to devour all babies newly born in that land. These demons were banished into the sea by the power of the *parittas*. Thenceforth the Burmese custom has prevailed to invite the monks to recite *Paritta Suttas* in the house of a newly born baby.

In early Pagan, the *paritta* spells were also used as means for the expiation of sins. It was taught that all guilts and sins need bring no retribution if the sinner recited an appropriate *paritta*, or he might request the monks to recite for him and to sprinkle the *paritta* water on his body for perfect purification.

To cite another instance, King Kyansitha of Pagan built up a new palace in the city and celebrated the event by holding elaborate ceremonies of recitation of the *Paritta Suttas*. It was in 1102 A.D., the Glass Palace Chronicle indicated that 4108 monks presided by the Elder Shin Arahant recited the *parittas*, poured the *paritta* holy water all around the newly built palace, and scattered the *paritta* sand all over the site. The *paritta* thread was also tied around the buildings as well as on the limbs of the people to protect unnecessary dangers in the new palace. Since then, the historical records have paid much attention to the importance of the recitation of *parittas* by monks as an essential ritual observed by the royal houses in Burma.

Nowadays every Burmese Buddhist family resort to the practice of the same rituals in the like manner. Usually, a *paritta* pavilion is constructed and a pot of water, a flower vase with Rose-apple (*Thabye*) leaves and some other flowers, a roll of thread, and a pot of clean sand are necessarily arranged in front of the altar of the Buddha. The thread is drawn round the interior of the pavilion, the end of which is twisted round the water pot and tied to the palm-leaf religious manuscripts or the altar of the Buddha. Sometimes the reciting monks hold in their hands the end of the thread. The extended thread held by them is passed on to the audience who face the altar. They must hold the thread while the monks are reciting *parittas* in unison.

When the recital is over, the profane water is converted into holy water; the ordinary thread and sand become sacred; the leaves of Rose-apple and flowers change their status and become supramundane objects.

Then the holy water, the sacred thread, the *paritta* sand and flowers are shared among the audience. The sanctified water is sprinkled on the body and the buildings, the sacred sand and flowers are scattered all over the compound, and the sacred thread is tied round the wrists or necks. All these observances are regarded as symbols of the protective power of the *parittas*.

Thus, in the Buddhist Burma, it becomes a well-esteemed practice to listen to the recital of the Dhamma, the doctrine of the Buddha, in order to avert dangers, to ward off the influence of malignant beings, to obtain protection and deliverance from evil, and to promote health, prosperity, welfare and well-being. No festival or function, whether religious or social, is complete without the recital of the *Paritta Suttas*. The ceremonies of Initiation and Ordination cannot be concluded without listening to the chanting of *parittas*. The pavilion especially constructed for such purposes is known as *Paritta-Maṇḍapa* – the Pavilion to listen to *paritta* recitation.

In the book of the Questions of King Milinda (1st century A.D.), a list of six *parittas* is mentioned: *Ratana*, *Khandha*, *Mora*, *Dhajagga*, *Āṭānāṭiya*, and *Aṅgulimāla Parittas*. The sanction of their utility is there made questionable. The dilemma is: the *parittas* were promulgated by the Glorious Lord Buddha. Now if a man may not escape death, the *paritta* is futile; if the *paritta* saves him, it is not true anymore that one cannot escape death.

As a matter of fact, the *Paritta Suttas*, *the Khandha* for example, had been prescribed by the Glorious Lord Buddha in the *Vinaya* texts – as a watch, a guard, a protection for one's self, for the use of the Monastic Order.

In general rule, the chanted formula consists of a profession of love towards all creatures, a prayer for the welfare of all beings. This specific profession of amity is no mere matter of pretty speech. It is highly imbued with psychical and emotional powers.

The asseveration of Truth (*saccakiriya*) is also another aspect of the work ascribed to the *Paritta Suttas*. The fact that Truth protects the devotee of the Dhamma, indicates the Buddhist belief in the recital of these *Paritta Suttas*. Indeed, *paritta* recital is a form of asseveration of truth which generates the power of protection and saving.

It is quite natural to clutch at any conceivable means that may avail to save, especially at the time of vital peril. Thus, the *paritta* rite is still prevalent in Burma as a cry for help in the hours of disaster, or sickness, or difficulty.

These *parittas* or protecting charms are not anti to Buddhist doctrine, but are in harmony with it. The agencies who have power to harm are blessed with good wishes, and suffused with an outgoing love. Even the most malignant spirits and beasts are looked upon as erring unfortunates on their age-long upward way, and they are capable of being doctored and softened by the effective power of compassionate love. The Buddhist's idea of the moral order reigning in the universe justifies him in the practice of the *paritta*.

If we consider the case of a patient, the physician's regular remedies are necessary as well as faith cure. Either means may avail if the patient's *kamma* for this life has not exhausted. The fervent recitals of the *parittas* as synergy of thought (psychic power) can possibly be an effective medicine no less than the material appliances of medical science. They are intended to range benign agencies on the side of the patient, and to keep away those that may harm.

The *parittas* have much of the power of prayer. In these the mighty powers and glories of the Lord Buddha, the truth of the Dhamma, and the virtues of all holy saints (*Arahats*) are called to mind and thus yield strength. The heart of unbounded love converts foes to friends, fear to courage, hatred to affection.

However, frankly speaking, *paritta* is not a protection to everybody. Just like medicine or food keep some people alive but kill others who consume too much of them, thus even life-giving drug or food may become poisonous by over-indulgence in it.

So also, there are three reasons for the failure of *paritta* to protect some people, the obstruction of *kamma* (*Kamma-kkhaya*) and obstruction of result of evil deeds (*Akusala vipāka*) and of disbelief (*Asaddhā*). That *paritta* which is a protection to beings loses its power by evil deeds done by those sinners themselves. Instead of helping, the recital sometimes may be futile to such non-believers. So, the *parittas* should be recited or should be listened most reverently and in full faith.

PARITTA AS BHĀVANĀ MEDITATION

To sum up, the recitation of *Paritta Suttas* is the act of Buddhist meditation-*bhāvanā*. Recollection of the glories and virtues of the Buddha, of the Dhamma, of the Saṅgha are (*Anussati Kammaṭṭhāna*), the meditation practices prescribed by Lord Buddha in *Abhidhammā Piṭaka* canon. It is therefore an act which accrues the auspicious merits promulgated in the *Mahā Maṅgala Sutta.*

1) Listening to the doctrines (*Kālena Dhamma Savanā*)

2) Discussion of the Dhamma (*Kālena Dhammasākacchā*)

3) Self-establishment (*Attasammāpaṇidhi*)

4) Mindfulness in the Dhamma (*Appamādo Dhammesu*) and others.

These auspices shall help the devotees to be happy everywhere, to be always successful and safe, the meritorious deeds done by means of *Paritta Kamma* shall positively yield the blessings to the faithful devotees (*Kusala Kamma Vipāko*). So, the recitation of *Paritta Sutta* is meant not only to avoid and overcome the dangers and calamities of this life, but also to eradicate all the defilements which are obstructing on the Path to Enlightenment – to Nibbāna.

RECITE AND WORK

For a Theravāda Burmese Buddhist, recitation of *Paritta Dhamma* alone is not enough to achieve all the aims and objects of his happy life; it is only a good verbal act (*Vacīkamma*) of a devotee. One must also strive hard physically (*Kāyakamma*) to attain the proposed goal. A bonafide Burmese Theravādin must think rightly (*Manokamma*) and plan correctly what to do prior to his verbal services, and then must operate diligently. Salvation through work, prayer, and faith should be the trichotomic salient feature of Burmese Buddhism. Physically, mentally and spiritually the Burmese Buddhist must develop himself to be eligible for the attainment of secular prosperity here in this life and for the supramundane bliss hereafter. A Burman shall discipline himself to purify his thinking, his morality and his view of life. Therefore, recitation of the suttas, discourses, and words of Lord Buddha is a part of, but not the whole of, the essential duty to be fulfilled by the devotee for his Enlightenment, for the attainment of *Nirvana*.

Though he utters much that is sensible,
if the heedless may be not a doer of the word.
He is like a cowherd counting the cows
of others, and has no part in the religious life.

Bahumpice samhita bhāsamāno
na takkaro hoti naro pamatto
gopo va gāvo gaṇayaṃ paresaṃ
na bhāgavā sāmaññassa hoti

Dhmp: Yamaka: 19

Though one should recite a hundred
stanzas composed of meaningless sentences,
Yet one Sentence of the Law is better,
which if a man hears he is at peace.

Yo ca gāthā sataṃ bhāse
anattha pada saṃhitā.
Ekaṃ dhammapadaṃ seyyo
Yaṃ sutvā upasammati.

Dhmp: Sahassa: 102

Indeed, the Words of the Buddha or the Dhamma are the guiding principles for the devotees to carry out their daily work properly. However, without practical work or labour nothing can be achieved completely in time.

It is you who must put forth exertion;
the Tathāgatas are only guides;
By meditation, those that enter upon
this Path win release from the bondage of Mara.

Tumhehi Kiccaṃ-ātappaṃ akkhātāro Tathāgatā

Dhmp: 276

Bring ye the Buddha–Word to pass;
Let not
This moment of the ages pass you by!
That moment lost, men mourn in misery.

Karotha Buddhavacanaṃ
Khaṇo vo mā upaccagā
Khanātitā hi socanti
nirayamhi samappitā.

Thera: 403

Rise up, rouse thee, Kātiyāna, seat thee crosslegged.
Be not filled with drowsiness. Watch and keep vigil.
Child of heedless race, let not the King of Mortals
By a simple trick o'ercome thee self-indulgent.

Uṭṭhehi, nisida, Kātiyana
Mā niddā bahulo ahu jāgarassu
Mā taṃ alasaṃ pamattabandhu
Kūṭeneva jinātu Maccurājā.

Thera: 411

Therefore, it is wisely suggested here that we think rightly, speak truly, and work diligently to attain whatever objective it may be, for the benefit of the individual as well as for the welfare of all mankind.

Come! For an instance! We shall recite the Discourse of Love (*Mettā Paritta Sutta*) and we shall practise to Love one and all others; to be able to abide happily in this present life and the next, to attain the Ultimate Happiness, Nibbāna.

May you all be free from dangers,

and enjoy your daily life happily!

Sao Htun Hmat Win

MAHĀ PARITTA PĀḶI
The Text of Great Protection

May veneration be dedicated to Him, the Almighty, the Most Infallible, and the Self-enlightened Supreme Buddha.

Invocation and Prayer

1) O deities, who are residing in the environs of various (ten thousand) universes, may you come here to this place, and listen to the sacred doctrine of the Lord of Sages, which can yield the divine bliss and perfect emancipation.

2) O deities, this is the right time to listen to the doctrine.

3) May our veneration be dedicated to Him, the Almighty, the Most Infallible, and the Self-enlightened Supreme Buddha.

4) Those who are tranquil and peaceful in mind, who have taken refuge in the three holy creeds, here in this world or in other spheres, the deities of terrestrial and celestial, who always are anxious to accrue the accumulation of merits.

   Those deities (and the King of gods) who are residing on royal Meru, the majestic golden mountain, and all those virtuous ones may come here in unity to listen to noble words of the Great Sage, which are the root cause of contentment.

5) The demons, the deities, and the Brahma gods in all universes (may rejoice in) whichever meritorious deeds we have done for the accomplishment of all enjoyments.

6) Having rejoiced in this sharing of merit, may all be comfortable and unanimous in His Teachings.

May all be free from negligence especially in the duties of protection.

7) May there always be prosperity in the religions as well as in the world.

May the deities always guard the religion as well as the world.

8) May all of you together with your own (fellow) retinues be happy.

May you together with all of your relative be painless and joyful.

9) May you take care in protecting from the dangers of tyrants, robbers, human enemies, inhuman beings, conflagration, flood, demons, tree-stumps, thorns, evil planets, village diseases, law-breakers, heretics, impious men, and of dangers from the wild elephants, horses, beasts, bulls, dogs, serpents, scorpions, copper-head snakes, panthers, bears, hyenas, boars, buffaloes, ogres, devils, etc. and also of dangers from various fears, various diseases and various disasters.

[1] MAṄGALA SUTTA
The Discourse on Auspices

The *Maṅgala Sutta* is sometimes highly esteemed by the Burman as *Mahāmaṅgala Sutta* (the Discourse on Great Auspices).

It is alleged to have been expounded by Lord Buddha when requested by a certain deity to explain to him what the ideal auspices really might be. Eventually, the Lord elaborated thirty-eight items of auspices which are to be approved as supreme. This discourse is the first and most famous of eleven *Paritta Suttas* prescribed in the Burmese Buddhism. The fifteen stanzas of the text in Pāḷi are learnt by heart and recited not only for protection from dangers, but as a mean to attain every problematic end in view of worldly affairs and supramundane realizations.

It has been usually chanted by the monks soon after they are honoured and served formally or informally by the lay devotees. And the faithful Buddhists believe that having listened to the recital of this discourse of Auspices, they would be undefeated in every respect, and would go in safety everywhere, now and forever from here to eternity.

This Sutta composed of fifteen stanzas, is the eminent generator of the Burmese spirit. It exhorts the social ethics and delivers the guiding principles which every Burman Buddhist shall observe in different stages of his daily life career.

Introduction

10) The meaning of the term "Auspice" had been speculated by gods and men for twelve years, however, they could not acquire the actual meaning of it. So, the discourse on thirty-eight auspices.

11) Which can eradicate all sins and evils, was expounded by the Supreme Deity (Buddha) for the benefit and welfare of the entire world. Oh thou! Let us recite this discourse on the Auspices now.

12) Thus, have I heard:

On one occasion the Glorious Lord was dwelling near Sāvatthi at the Jeta's grove in the pleasaunce of Anāthapiṇḍika. Thereupon, a certain deity whose surpassing radiance illuminating the entire Jeta grove, approached the Glorious Lord quite late at night. He respectfully saluted the Lord and stood at one side. And so, standing, he addressed the Glorious One in verse thus,

13) Many gods and men yearning for happiness have speculated about the problems of Auspices.

Please explain to me what supreme Auspices really are.

14) Not to associate with the foolish (1); but to associate with the wise (2); and to honour those worthy of honour (3) – this is the auspice supreme.

The Minor Readings; P.T.S. tr. Bhikkhu Ñāṇamoli; Luzac and Co. Ltd. London, 1960. pp.2–4.

The Good Omen Discourse.

The Illustrator of Ultimate Meaning: P.T.S. Chapter V. pp. 94–172.

15) To dwell in suitable locality (4); to be endowed with merits accrued in the past (5) and to establish oneself rightfully (6) – this is the auspice supreme.

16) To have immensity of knowledge (7); to acquire skill in sciences (8); to be well-trained in discipline (9); and to have words well spoken (10) – this is the auspice supreme.

17) To serve thy parents (11); to support thy wife and children (12); to be engaged in peaceful occupations (13) – this is the auspice supreme.

18) Generosity (14); lawful-conduct (15); to support thy relatives (16); and to perform faultless actions (17); – this is the auspice supreme.

19) To abstain from evil (18); to refrain from sin (19); to restrain from intoxicating drinks (20); and to be diligent in Laws (21) – this is the auspice supreme.

20) Reverence (22); modesty (23); contentment (24); gratitude towards the grateful (25); timely audition of the doctrines (26) – this is the auspice supreme.

21) Patience (27); obedience (28); to visit the monks (29); and the timely discussions of the doctrines (30) – this is the auspice supreme.

22) Ascetic practices (31); chastity (32); to discern the noble truths (33); to realize the Nirvana (34) – this is the auspice supreme.

23) The mind which is touched by the eight vicissitudes of life does not move (35); be free from anxiety (36); be stainlessly pure (37); and be perfectly secure (38) – this is the auspice supreme.

Maṅgala = auspice, good omen, luck, blessing, beatitude, fortune.

24) Those who have done such like auspices are unvanquished (successful) everywhere, and attain bliss (happiness) everywhere. To them these are the auspices supreme.

The end of the Maṅgala Sutta.

[2] RATANA SUTTA
The Discourse on Precious Jewels

A Historical Sketch

During the lifetime of our Lord Buddha the city of Vesāli was afflicted by famine, which killed thousands of poverty-stricken families. Due to the presence of decaying corpses the evil spirits haunted the city, and led to inevitable pestilence. Plagued by these three perils of famine, devils and pestilence, the Vesālians sought the help of the Buddha who was then dwelling at Rājagaha.

Moved by deep compassionate love, Lord Buddha marched to the plagued city of Vesāli, followed by hundreds of monks including the Venerable Ānanda. No sooner had the Lord arrived at the city, then the torrential rains poured down and swept away the putrefying dead bodies. So, the city was cleansed and the atmosphere became purified.

Then the Buddha delivered the Discourse on Precious Jewels to the Venerable Ānanda and instructed him to tour the city reciting the discourse as a means of protection to the citizens of Vesāli.

The Venerable Ānanda obeyed the command and sprinkled the holy water from the alms-bowl of the Lord, to banish the evil spirits consequently and eventually the pestilence subsided.

Ratana = precious jewel, gem, preciousness.

The Minor Readings: P.T.S. tr Bhikkhu Ñāṇamoli, Luzag, and Co. Ltd. London 1960, pp 4–6, The Jewel Discourse.

The Illustrator of Ultimate Meaning: P.T.S. Chapter VI pp 172–222.

Thereafter, the Venerable Ānanda reported the events promptly to the Lord, who was awaiting his arrival at the City Hall of Vesāli. Then again, Lord Buddha recited the same discourse and explained the intrinsic value of the text to the assembled disciples. Thus, the recitation of the discourse had been approved by the Lord and the assembly.

According to the standard Burmese Version, this discourse is composed of twenty-one blank verses including the introductory prelude. This sutta is usually treated as an exegesis of the virtues of the three precious jewels namely, Buddha, Dhamma and Saṅgha.

Introduction

25) Retrospecting all these virtues of Lord Buddha such as: commencing from the time of his Noble Vow (pledged in the presence of Lord Dipaṅkarā, to become a Buddha) the Tathāgata had fulfilled all the thirty (*Pāramitas*) Perfections, viz: the ten ordinary Perfections, the ten (*Upapāramitas*) superior Perfections, and the ten (*Paramattha Pāramitas*) supreme Perfections;

the five Great Sacrifices;

the three modes of Practice, viz: the practice for the welfare of the world, for the welfare of kinsmen and relatives, and for the benefit of his attainment of Buddhahood;

and that he had been naturally conceived in his mother's womb in this last existence;

his nativity, the Great Renunciation, the experience of Austerity;

the Conquest upon (five types of) Death (Māra)

being seated under the Bo tree; the Discernment of Omniscient Wisdom;

expounding the sermon of the Rotating of the Wheel of Law (*Dhammacakkappavattana sutta*);

and the nine supramundane laws:

Reverend Ānanda the Elder, did the protective recitation throughout the three watches of the night,

within the three walls of the city of Vesālī.

Having established such a sympathetic mind as Reverend Ānanda did,

26) the glory of which had been accepted by the deities who have assembled in the hundred-thousand-crores of universes.

And in the city of Vesālī.

27) By the power of which the three types of disasters, that broke out due to epidemic diseases, inhuman beings, and famine

were also eradicated promptly, Oh thou! Let us recite this discourse of protection.

28) Whatever beings are assembled here so be they terrestrial or celestial May all beings have peaceful mind,

And also listen attentively to these words.

29) Therefore, O beings, listen closely. Radiate lovingkindness to your fellow beings.

By day and by night, they bring offerings to you

Therefore, protect them well with diligence.

30) Whatever treasure there be either here or in the world beyond;

whatever precious jewel there be in the heavenly abodes;

none is there equal to the Perfect One.

This precious jewel (holiness) is the Enlightened One.

By this asseveration of the Truth, may there be the perfect bliss.

31) That Cessation, Detachment, and holy Immortality

has been realized by the perfectly meditated Sakyan-Sage

There is no equal ideal to this Dhamma

This holy jewel indeed lies in the Dhamma.

By this asseveration of the Truth, may there be the perfect bliss.

32) The Supreme Enlightened One extolled the path of purity

calling it the Concentration which yields infallible result immediately

No equal is there to such concentration

this holy jewel indeed lies in the Dhamma

By this asseveration of the Truth, may there be the perfect bliss.

33) The eight persons are extolled by holy men;

And they constituted four pairs, they are the disciples of the Sublime Lord worthy of offerings.

Gifts offered to them yield rich results.

This holy jewel, indeed lies in the Saṅgha

By this asseveration of the Truth, may there be the perfect bliss.

34) Striving well with a steadfast mind,

they are liberated during the Dispensation of Gotama Buddha.

They have attained the highest state, having encountered the immortality.

They enjoy the perfect peace which they obtained without obligation.

This precious jewel (holiness) is in the Saṅgha.

By this asseveration of the truth may there be the perfect bliss.

35) As a post deep planted in the earth stands
unshaken by the winds blast from four quarters.
So also, I declare the righteous man is unshaken
who sees the Noble Truths through discriminating wisdom.

This precious jewel (holiness) is in the Saṅgha.

By this asseveration of the truth may there be the perfect bliss.

36) Those who develop the Noble Truths well expounded by the Lord of Proof of Wisdom
even though they may be exceedingly heedless;
Still, they do not take an eighth existence (in the realm of Kāmabhūmi).

This precious jewel (holiness) is in the Saṅgha.

By this asseveration of the truth may there be the perfect bliss.

37) Simultaneously with his accomplishment of Insight
Three mental aspects are abandoned
namely individualism, doubt, and Indulgence in futile rites and rituals,
and other defilements if there be any.

38) He is also emancipated from the four states of deprivation

And can no more commit the six major sins.

This precious jewel (holiness) is in the Saṅgha.

By this asseveration of the truth may there be the perfect bliss.

39) Though he may still do evil deed physically, verbally or mentally

Yet he cannot conceal it.

Since it has been promulgated that such concealing is impossible for one Who has seen the Path.

This precious jewel (holiness) is in the Saṅgha.

By this asseveration of the truth may there be the perfect bliss.

40) Just like (the glory of) the woodland groves crowned with blossoms

in the early heat of the warm summer month,

even so the glory of the sublime (Dhamma) doctrine was expounded for the supreme prosperity leading towards Nibbāna.

This precious jewel (holiness) is in the Buddha.

By this asseveration of the truth may there be the perfect bliss.

41) The Glorious One, who knows the glory, delivers the glory, brings the glory

and is the peerless expounded the glorious doctrine.

This precious jewel (holiness) is in the Buddha.

By this asseveration of the truth may there be the perfect bliss.

42) Their former (*kamma*) is exhausted and the new one arises no more.

The lust for future-becoming is detached.

The seed germ (of rebirth) has exhausted and they have no more desire for regrowing.

As this lamp-flame extinguishes away, the wise men pass away (into) Nibbāna.

This precious jewel (holiness) is in the Saṅgha.

By this asseveration of the truth may there be the perfect bliss.

43) Whatever beings are assembled here, so be they terrestrial or celestial, come, let us worship the Buddha; (the Perfect One), who is honoured by gods and men.

May there be the perfect bliss.

44) Whatever beings are assembled here, so be they terrestrial or celestial, come, let us worship the Dhamma, (Doctrine); (the Perfect One) which is honoured by gods and men.

May there be the perfect bliss.

45) Whatever beings are assembled here, so be they terrestrial or celestial, come, let us worship the Saṅgha, (Order); (the Perfect One) which is honoured by gods and men.

May there be the perfect bliss.

The end of the Ratana Sutta.

[3] METTĀ SUTTA
The Discourse on Lovingkindness

A Historical Sketch

Lord Buddha was then residing at Sāvatthi in the pleasaunce of Anāthapiṇḍika and a group of monks received permission from the Lord to meditate in a distant forest during their retreat for the rainy season. The monks took shelter under huge trees as temporary residence and engaged themselves intensively in the practice of meditation.

The tree deities inhabiting this forest could not stay in their tree-abodes which were above the monks, for the monks were imbued with spiritual power due to meditation and they had to come down to stay on the ground. So, the deities were very much annoyed and frustrated and when they realized that the monks would spend the whole rainy season there, they tried to scare the monks away during the nights. They purposely harassed the monks in various ways.

Living under such impossible conditions for some time, the disturbed meditators rushed back to the Buddha and informed about their difficulties. So, the Buddha advised them to recite the text of Lovingkindness and to radiate the spirit of Love to all sentient beings. Encouraged by this media, the meditators returned to the forest and practised in accordance with the instructions to permeate the entire atmosphere with the radiant thoughts of Love. The tree-gods were very much pleased to be affected by this power of love and thenceforth let the monks stay there to meditate peacefully without any further disturbances.

This discourse, as a matter of fact, is the Buddhist doctrine of Love, which promulgates the method of practice to disseminate Love in order to attain Purity and Peace, to realize finally the Perfect Emancipation.

This sutta is composed of twelve stanzas, with two introductory verses beautifully set by the learned elder-monks of Burma.

Introduction

46) Due to the glorious power of this discourse on Love, spirits dare not disclose the frightful sights.
One who devotes to himself this doctrine day and night diligently.

47) sleeps soundly and does not see any nightmare when asleep.
Oh thou! Let us recite this doctrine, endowed with such and other merits.

48) He who is clever in the benefaction and who has anticipated in the attainment of the state of Perfect Tranquility
must work to be efficient, right, upright, discussable, gentle, and humble,

49) Contented, well-bred,
less responsible, of fugal livelihood, serene in faculties, prudent,
modest, not hanker after the families,

The Minor Readings; P.T.S. tr. *The Lovingkindness Discourse* pp. 10–11
The Illustrator of Ultimate Meaning; P.T.S. tr. Ch. IX. PP 265–294.
Mettā = love, affection, benevolence, Eros, agape amour, lovingkindness.

50) He must not commit even the slightest Sin for which the wise men might censure.

He must contemplate thus: may all sentient beings be cheerful

and be endowed with happy secured life.

51) Whatever breathing beings there may be

the frail ones or the firm creatures, with no exception tall or stout, short or medium-sized, thin or fat,

52) Those which are seen or those unseen, those who are dwelling far or near those who are already born or those still seeking to become yet,

May all these beings be endowed with happy-life.

53) Let not one be angry with another, let him not despise anyone in any place

By means of physical and verbal provocation or by frustrated enmity,

Let one not wish another's suffering.

54) Just like a mother would protect her baby,

the only child, with her life, even so towards all beings

let one cultivate the (*Agape*) boundless spirit of love.

55) Let him radiate the boundless rays of Love

towards the entire world,

to the above, below, and across unhindered,

without malice and enmity.

56) While standing, walking, sitting, reclining, as long as he be awake without sloth,

Let him devote himself to this mindfulness.

This is called in this religion as "*Noble Living*" (*Holy life*).

57) If the meditator, without falling into wrong view (egoism), be virtuous,
and endowed with perfect insight, has expelled passion in sensual desires,
he will surely come never again to be born in any womb.

The end of the Mettā Sutta.

[4] KHANDHA SUTTA
The Discourse on Protection of the Aggregates

This *Khandha Paritta* is the Buddhist spell, or wardrune, an example of Apotropaic Buddhism in Burma. According to the *Vinaya Piṭaka* literature in *Cūḷavagga* text, this is allegedly composed by Lord Buddha when a certain monk in Sāvatthi died of snakebite. The Buddha declared that this would not have happened had that monk let his love radiate over the four royal breeds of serpents and all the monks were advised to protect from snakes by means of love through the reciting of *Khandha Paritta* which the Lord then composed for them.

The same *paritta* is mentioned also in the *Jātaka* stories, the *Khandha Vaṭṭa Jātaka*. According to the story, the Bodhisatta (Buddha-to-be) was an ascetic in a previous birth who heard his friend ascetics complaining about the dangers they encountered from snakes. He therefore instructed them to recite the spell or wardrune in Pāḷi, known as *Khandha Paritta*.

This *paritta* is nowadays recited for protection not only against dangerous snakes, for which it was originally composed, but even from other frightful creatures as well, including reptiles, scorpions, centipedes, spiders, lizards, rats, and mice.

The peculiar phenomenon of this discourse is that Lord Buddha declared openly the power of reciting for personal safety, for personal preservation, and for personal protection (*Parittaṃ*). This *Paritta Sutta* is composed according to the Burmese version, eight stanzas in Pāḷi.

Vinaya Piṭaka. Cūlavagga. P. 101–102.
Jātaka, the Khandha Vaṭṭa Jātaka.

Introduction

58) Just like the divine charms and divine drugs,
this discourse of Khandha nullifies the baneful poison
and the other perils of all the highly poisonous creatures.

59) In this scope of (Buddha's) jurisdiction everywhere,
always, for all beings,
and by all means, this discourse does prevent (the disasters).
Oh thou! Let us recite this preventive discourse now.

60) May my love be with Virūpakkha snakes; with Erāpatha snakes, may there be my love.
May my love be with Chavyāputta snakes;
with Kaṇhāgotamaka snakes may there he my love too.

61) With footless-creatures may there be my love.
May my love be with bipeds;
with quadrupeds may there be my love;
May my love be with multipeds.

62) May the foot-less hurt me not;
May the bipeds not hurt me; the quadrupeds may not hurt me;
the multipeds may hurt me not.

63) All the sentient creature and all breathing ones,
all beings without exception,
all may see the happy sights,
and may not befall into any sin.

64) The Buddha is infinite:
Infinite is the Dhamma;
The Saṅgha is infinite;
Finite and measurable are creeping things;
snakes, scorpions, centipedes, spiders, lizards, and rats.

65) I have guarded myself; I have protected myself;
Let all evil beings recede.
Here I salute to the Glorious One.
And to the Seven Buddhas do I honour.

The end of the Khandha Sutta.

[5] MORA SUTTA

The Discourse on the Peacock's Prayer

A Historical Sketch

The birth story of the Buddha as a golden peacock was narrated by the Lord at *Jetavana* monastery when it was reported that a disciple monk had been enchanted by a woman.

Our Buddha-to-be was once born as a golden peacock, residing on the golden hill of Daṇḍaka in the Himalaya mountains. When day dawned, the golden peacock used to sit upon the summit watching the rising sun, composed a prayer to protect himself safe in his feeding pasture. He then recited worshipping the past Buddhas and all their virtuous glories. Uttering this charm to protect himself from dangers, he went afeeding.

In the evening when the sun went down, the bird came back to the hilltop on which he rested to watch the setting sun, and he meditated to utter another prayer to protect him from dangers during the night time. He then went to sleep.

There was then a hunter who had seen him and told the wonders of the bird to his son. At that time queen Khemā of Beṇares had a dream who pushed her to demand the king to bring the golden peacock to the palace. She wanted to listen to the discourse of the bird. The king sent the hunter to catch the bird. But by the power of the prayer and charm the snare would not work to catch him. After seven years the unsuccessful hunter died followed by the demise of the queen.

The Jātaka Vol. 2. (No. 159) P.23.

There upon the old king was angry with the bird and left an inscription saying that whoever eats the flesh of the golden peacock shall ever be young and immortal. So, six successive rulers of the kingdom attempted to capture the bird but all in vain.

The seventh successor king sent a clever hunter who had a charming peahen which could sing very sweetly. Early in the morning the hunter set up the snare with the peahen which sang very enchantingly before the golden bird could recite his usual prayer and charm. The bird was tempted and approached her, and was caught in the snare. The happy hunter caught hold of the golden bird and hurried back to the palace to present it to the king.

The king was delighted at the bird's golden beauty and placed the bird on a royal seat to exchange a dialogue with him.

The golden peacock related the story of his previous life as a pious king in the same kingdom and also explained the power of his prayer and charm to the king. He also advised the king to excavate the golden chariot from the royal lake to prove his narration. When all the truths were revealed, the bird was released to fly back to the golden hill of Daṇḍaka. And the story ends happily.

Hence this *Mora Sutta* has been chanted as a charm or wardrune to protect the subjects from snares or to be released safely if arrested by the enemies. It is usually uttered by Burman Buddhist to keep the entire family safe and sound throughout the entire day and night.

According to the Burmese version of the *Mahā Paritta Pāḷi* text, this sutta is composed of six stanzas only.

Introduction

66) The Great Being (the Buddha-to-be) was born as a peacock,

fulfilling the necessary requirements for obtaining Enlightenment,

and having arranged protection for himself by means of this protective discourse.

Him, the Great Being, although the hunters

67) Strived for quite a long time,

they were not able to capture.

This was described by Lord Buddha as an Exalted Charm.

Oh thou! Let us recite this protective discourse.

68) There he rises, the thousand-eyed king,

Making the world bright with his golden light.

Thee I worship, oh glorious wing, with thy golden light, making the world bright.

Keep me safe, I pray, through the coming day.

69) The saints, the righteous, wise in the entire holy lore,

They may protect me and to them I adore

Honour be to the wise, honour be to wisdom,

To freedom, and to those who had achieved freedom.

Having made this protection, the peacock went about to seek food.

70) There he sets, the thousand-eyed king, He that makes the world bright with his golden light.

Thee I worship, oh glorious wing, with thy golden light making the world bright.

Through the night, till the next day;

Keep me safe, I pray.

71) The saints, the righteous, wise in the entire holy lore,
They may protect me, and to them I adore.
Honour be to the wise, honour be to wisdom.
To freedom, and to those who had achieved freedom.
Having made this protection,
that peacock rested happily at home.

The end of the Mora Sutta.

Vaṭṭaka Sutta = *Vaṭṭaka Jātaka.*
Cariyā Piṭaka P. 98.
The Jātaka No. 35. Vol. I. P. 90.

[6] VAṬṬA SUTTA
The Discourse of the Quail's Asseveration

Once, Lord Buddha went on his morning round for alms through a certain hamlet in Magadha. On his return after his breakfast, accompanied by his disciples came to a place where a great jungle-fire broke out; the disciples fled towards the Lord and saw him standing untouched by the raging flame. When they exclaimed and praised Him on His miraculous powers the Lord explained to them that it was the power of a previous "Act of Truth" which he had performed in his former life as a quail. Since then, in this spot no fire will burn throughout the whole of this aeon. This miracle was one which would endure for an aeon.

In his previous birth as a quail, there broke out a forest-fire. Fearing for their lives all creatures, including his own parents fled away leaving only the helpless baby-quail in the nest. The young bird was then too young to fly or to walk and he was forsaken all alone. Thereupon he meditated on the efficacy of the past Buddhas as well as the efficacy of Truth. He then performed an Oath of Truth and wished that the fire may recede. The angry flame calmed down and waived the spot of sixteen hectors (lengths) just like a burning torch had been dipped into the water. The fire was extinguished by the miracle of the Oath uttered by the baby-quail. As this spot will remain for the whole aeon untouched by any fire, this miracle is called an aeon-miracle.

This *Paritta Sutta* of six stanzas in Pāḷi, is therefore recited in Burma to protect and prevent from dangers of conflagration and forest fire.

Introduction

72) By the power of this discourse, the forest-fire passed over the Great Being (the Buddha-to-be) who was born as a quail, fulfilling the necessary requirements for obtaining Enlightenment.

73) Oh thou! Let us recite this discourse, which was expounded by the Saviour of the world (the Buddha) to the Elder Sāriputta, and which will last for aeons, being endowed with mighty powers.

74) There's saving merit in virtue in this world;
Truth, purity of life, and compassion too,
Thereby, I'll work a matchless Act of Truth.

75) Remembering the Law's might, and reflecting
On those who triumphed in the days gone by,
Depending on the might of truth,
an Act of Truth I wrought.

76) With wings I can't fly, with feet I can't walk,
gone away my parents, here I am alone.
Oh Forest-fire, please recede.

77) I wrought my Act of Truth, and therewith
The sheet of blazing fire waived for sixteen hectares
Unscathed - like flames by water, met and quenched.
There is no equal to my Truth asseveration.
This is my perfection of Truth.

The end of the Vaṭṭa Sutta.

[7] DHAJAGGA SUTTA
The Discourse on the Crest of Banners

The *Dhajagga Sutta* is based on a tale narrated by the Buddha in the Book of the Kindred Sayings (*Saṃyutta Nikāya*) of *Sakka Saṃyutta*. When the gods (*devas*) and the titans (*asuras*) were engaged in battle, Sakka, the king of the gods, encouraged his soldiers that should they become frightened they need only look up at the crest of his banner, or the banners of other three chieftans of gods, Pajāpati, Varuṇa, and lsāna. Then the arising fear, panic, and creeping of the flesh will be overcome. But this act may or may not help because Sakka, though may he be king of the gods, is yet timid and given to panic, and is not yet free from passion, hatred, and ignorance. Hence, the Lord instructed his disciples to remember the Buddha, the Doctrine and the Order according to the extolled virtues of each of these three precious jewels. If the monks do so, the Lord promised, any fear, panic, creeping of the flesh that will have arisen will be overcome. Because the Buddha, unlike Sakka, is Supremely Enlightened, is free form passion, hatred ignorance. He is without timidity or panic or fright, and He does not flee.

This *paritta* becomes very important the Burmese Buddhist rituals and monastic educational lessons. This *paritta* typically consists of scriptural passages of an entire chapter from *Saṃyutta Nikāya*. The most famous and short Buddhist spell is the recitation of the collection of the three Virtues the Buddha, the Dhamma and the Saṅgha which is the core essence of this *paritta*. The stanzas (*gāthā*) were originally recited by the Buddha following. His narration of a martial story as briefly mentioned above. But now they are used as protection in battle and in time of war.

Even when treating a patient, Burmese indigenous doctors recite the Virtues to empower the medicine to be potent. Some criminal and political prisoners also recite this spell as a way of obtaining their release. To generate the spiritual power of one self the Virtues are recited analytically while telling the rosary beads.

The Buddha, in the original sutta, prescribes their use merely as a means for overcoming fear. If, he promises the monks, any of the Three Jewels are contemplated with reference to their respective Virtues, fear, panic, and creeping of the flesh that will have arisen, will be entirely overcome. To have full faith in the three Precious Jewels, that is, to equip oneself with sound confidence and ardent courage in carrying out the religious duties and practices is the main essence of this discourse.

M.E, Spiro: *Buddhism and Society* — pp. 263. 264. 265.

Introduction

78) Just even by recollecting this discourse, the creatures get the foothold even in the sky, by all means, just like on the ground.

79) The number of those who had emancipated from the network of all dangers, created by devils, robbers, thieves, and others, is indeed innumerable. Oh thou! Let us recite this protective discourse now.

80) Thus I have heard:

The Exalted One once, stayed at the Jetavana, in Sāvatthi, in the pleasaunce of Anāthapiṇḍika.

There and then he addressed the disciples on this incident.

81) "Long ago, bhikkhus, a battle was raging between the gods and the titans. Then Sakka, ruler of the gods, addressed the Thirty-three gods, saying: 'If in you, dear sirs, when you are gone onto battle, fear, panic, and creeping of the flesh should arise, look up at the crest of my banner.

If you do so, any fear, panic, and creeping of the flesh that will have arisen will be overcome.

82) If you look not up to the crest of my banner, look up at that of Pajāpati, king of the gods, ...

83) or at that of Varuṇa, king of the gods, ...

84) Or at that of lsāna, king of the gods and any fear, panic, and creeping of the flesh that will have arisen will be overcome.'"

85) Now, bhikkhus, in them that look up to the crest of one or other of these four banners, any fear, panic, and

---

The Book of Kindred Sayings Ch. 11. p. 282–283.The Top of the Banner.

creeping of the flesh that has arisen may be overcome, or again it may not.

86) And why is this? Because Sakka, ruler of the gods, is not purged of passions, hatred, or ignorance, is timid, given to panic, to fright, to running away.

87) But I say thus unto you, bhikkhus:

If in you when you have gone into forests, to the roots of trees, to empty places, fear, panic, and creeping of the flesh should arise, do you in that hour only call me to mind and think:

88) This Exalted One is able, supremely enlightened, proficient in knowledge and in conduct, the Blessed One, understands the world, peerless tamer and driver of the hearts of men, the Master of gods and men, the Buddha, the Exalted One

89) For if you so call me to mind, bhikkhus, any fear, panic, and creeping of the flesh that will have arisen will be overcome.

90) And if you cannot call me to mind, call to mind the Dhamma and think:

91) Well proclaimed by the Exalted One is the Dhamma relating to the present, immediate in its results, inviting and challenging all, giving guidance, appealing to each, to be understood by the wise.

92) For if you so call the Dhamma to mind, your fear, panic, and creeping of the flesh will be overcome.

93) And if you cannot call the Dhamma to mind, then call to mind the Order, and think:

94) Well-practised is the Exalted One's Order of Disciples, practised in integrity, in intellectual methods in right

lines of action — to with the four pairs, the eight groups of persons: this is the Exalted One's Order or Disciples, worthy of offerings, oblations, gifts, salutations, the world's peerless field for merit.

95) For if you so call the Order to mind, your fear, panic, and creeping of the flesh will be overcome.

96) And why is this? Because the Tathāgata, bhikkhus, is *Arahant*, Supremely Enlightened, purged of passion, hatred, and ignorance, without timidity or panic or fright, and fleeth not.

97) Thus said the Exalted One and the Blessed One so saying, the Master spoke yet further:

98) Whenever in forest or in leafy shade or lonely empty places you abide,
Call to your mind, bhikkhus, the Enlightened One;
No fear, no sense of peril will you know.

99) Or if you cannot on the Buddha think:
The most senior of the world, the Bull of men —
Then call the Norm to mind, the well-taught guide.

100) Or if you cannot think upon the Law —
The well-taught doctrine wherein guidance lies —
Then turn your thoughts to the Fraternity,
Unrivalled field where men may sow good deeds.

101) If you in Buddha, Law, and Order thus refuge take,
Fear, panic, and creeping of the flesh will never rise.

The end of the Dhajagga Sutta.

[8] ĀṬĀNĀṬIYA SUTTA
The Discourse on Āṭānāṭiya

On one occasion, Lord Buddha was staying on the Vulture's Peak near Rājagaha. And four great kings, the guardian spirits of four quarters in the celestial regions, came to tell the Buddha that there were many demons in the land who neither believing in the Buddha nor abiding by the Five Precepts, frightened and attacked the disciple-monks and lay devotees who retire to lonely places for meditation.

Therefore, the great King Vessavaṇṇa (or Kuvera) wanted to present the *Āṭānāṭa Paritta* to the Lord that it may be recited to make the displeased demons to be pleased, and consequently the monks, nuns, lay devotees may be at ease, guarded, protected and unharmed.

The Lord Buddha gave consent by his silence to approve the recitation of the said discourse. So, King Vessavaṇṇa recited this *Paritta Sutta*.

Then the four great kings departed. When the night had passed the Buddha addressed the monks to learn the *Āṭānāṭa Paritta* by heart, to constantly use it, and to bear it in mind.

This *Āṭānāṭa Paritta* pertains to the welfare of mankind and by virtue of it all the disciples and lay devotees can live at ease, guarded, protected and unharmed.

According to the commentary, King Vessavaṇṇa had a town called *Āṭānāṭa* where the four great kings of the celestial regions assembled and recited this *paritta*. Hence this discourse is known as *Āṭānāṭiya Sutta*.

Dialogues of the Buddha. Part III; Vol. IV. S.B.E. P. 189–190.
The ward rune of *Āṭānāṭa.*

The ancient Burmese monks who were experts in Pāḷi language composed thirty stanzas of this sutta based upon six verses in the original text mentioned in *Digha Nikāya, Pāthikavagga, Āṭānāṭa Sutta*, concluding with an original verse from Dhammapada Pāḷi (409).

Introduction

102) In order that the hostile inhuman beings, who are always evil-doers and who do not have faith in this well esteemed religion of the Lord (Buddha)

103) may not injure the four social classes and may protect the society from dangers. the Almighty Hero has expounded this discourse of protection. Oh thou! Let us recite this *Āṭānāṭiya Sutta* now.

104) Homage to Vipassi Buddha, possessed of the eyes of enlightenment and of glory.

And Homage to Sikhi Buddha, the most compassionate towards all beings.

105) Homage also to Vessabhū Buddha, washed clean from all defilements and endowed with ascetic spirit.

Homage to Kakusandha Buddha too, the conqueror of the army of Death (Māra)

106) Homage to Koṇāgamana Buddha, who had abandoned all evils and lived the holy life.

Homage also to Kassapa Buddha, who had been emancipated from all defilements.

107) Homage to Buddha Gotama, whose body shined with radiating halo, the son of Sakyan and with splendourous

glory, who expounded this doctrine which eradicates all sufferings.

108) Whosoever have extinguished the flames of passion in this world as they have seen thoroughly the natural phenomena as they really are.

These persons never slander; but they are noble, and free from fear.

109) They worship Gotama Buddha, benefactor of gods and men, endowed with knowledge and good conduct, noble and fearless.

110) These seven and other hundred crores of self-enlightened Buddhas are all equally peerless ones.

All Buddhas are powerful ones.

111) All are endowed with ten strengths; they are equipped with courage. All these Buddhas admitted to be the knowers of supreme state of Enlightenment.

112) These Buddhas expound bravely to the audience like the Lion-roar; they propagate the Noble Wheel of Law in the world which cannot be done by ordinary worldlings.

113) These Patrons are equipped with eighteen virtues of the Buddha's Dhamma. They are born with thirty-two major characteristics and eighty minor characteristics of the great man.

114) All these Buddhas are noble sages who shine with the surrounding halo of about the length of one stretched arm. These Buddhas are all Omniscient Ones; and are Conquerors of Māra (Death) who have uprooted the defilements.

115) They all are endowed with immense radiation light, of almighty power, of infinite wisdom, and of immutable strength.

They are most compassionate and industrious benefactors of all beings.

116) They all are the Islands, the Lords, the Foot-holds, the Protectors, and the Secured Haven of the creatures. The Transcendental Goals, the Relatives, the Glorious Saviours, the Refuges, and the Well-wishers.

117) They all are revered by the world of gods and men.

I worship the feet of these Supreme Ones with my head.

118) I worship these Tathāgatas by means of word and thought-always; even when I am lying, sitting, standing or walking.

119) The Buddhas, the peace-makers may always protect you to be happy.

By these Buddhas, may you be protected so that you may, be liberated from all calamities.

120) May you be emancipated from all diseases.

May you be free from all scorching worries.

May you overcome all the enemies. And may you be blissful.

121) By the power of their truth, virtue, patience, loving kindness and might, they may also protect us to be healthy and happy.

122) In the eastern region there are powerful great deities (*bhūtas*).

They may also protect us to be healthy and happy.

123) In the southern region, there are great powerful gods (*devas*)
They may also protect us to be healthy and happy.

124) In the western region there are great powerful dragon snakes (*nāgās*)
They may also protect us to be healthy and happy.

125) In the northern region there are great powerful ogres (*genii yakkhas*).
They may also protect us to be healthy and happy.

126) King Dhataraṭṭha in the east,
King Virūḷhaka in the south,
King Virūpakkha in the west,
King Kuvera in the north,

127) These four great kings are famous guardian spirits of the world.
They may also protect us to be healthy and happy.

128) There are great powerful gods and dragons, residing in the sky and on the earth.
They may also protect us to be healthy and happy.

129) There are some powerful deities residing within the jurisdiction of this religion.
They may also protect us to be healthy and happy.

130) May all the dangers be eradicated.
May worry and illness be dispelled.
May the calamities do not occur to you.
May you be blissful and long-lived.

131) To those who are endowed with the nature of piety and who always revere to the elders, these four boons shall prosper; namely longevity, beauty, happiness and strength.

The end of the Āṭānāṭiya Sutta.

[9] AṄGULIMĀLA SUTTA
The Act of Truth by Reverend Aṅgulimāla

Ahiṃsaka Kumāra was born in the family of Brahmin — the chaplain of King Kosala and was known in his young age as the Son of Mantānī. He was educated at the Taxila University and the Rector asked him to collect one thousand fingers as a qualifying test. So, the lad killed many men to cut the fingers which he made a garland hanging around his neck. Hence, he became notorious as the Robber with a garland of fingers — *Aṅgulimāla Cora*.

Eventually the robber had collected the required fingers except the last one. So, he decided to cut the last finger from anyone he saw that day. King Kosala publicly notified that the royal army was going to annihilate the robber. Hearing this, Mantānī, the mother of the robber, hurried to her son to warn him. But the determined robber chased after his mother to cut her finger.

Now the most Compassionate Buddha saved the life of the helpless mother by standing between the runner and the chaser at the risk of His life.

When the robber saw the Buddha, he changed his mind from chasing his own mother and attempted to seize the Buddha. But the Buddha performed a miracle so that the chasing robber could not catch up with the slowly walking Buddha. Realizing the impossibility of the glory of the Buddha, Aṅgulimāla robber became a convert and was ordained as a monk. Thus, he became a disciple by the name of Reverend

Aṅgulimāla who worked intensively and soon became an *Arahanta* (saint).

One day Arahanta Aṅgulimāla saw a pregnant woman in difficult labour of child birth and reported the condition to the Buddha. So, the Buddha advised him to perform an oath of truth by declaring that he had not intentionally killed any life from the time he had become an Ariyan monk. This is a magical means for saving both lives of the mother and the new child. He did so and the lives of two beings were saved by this *paritta*.

Since then, the Burmese people used to bless the water by reciting this *paritta* of three stanzas and sprinkle on the head of the pregnant woman who is having difficulty in childbirth. And usually, it works well.

This is evidence that the Compassionate Buddha could convert a robber, who was killing thousands of lives, to become a saint who could save innumerable lives of mothers and children.

Introduction

132) Even the water that rinsed the seat of the Elder who recited this discourse of protection did eradicate all the dangerous difficulties.

133) That very *paritta* discourse has the power to accomplish the labour of childbirth healthily.

This is the *Paritta Sutta* which had been expounded by Lord of the worlds to Reverend Aṅgulimāla the great magical power of which may last long for the entire aeon.

Oh thou! Let us recite this discourse of protection.

134) "I, sister, in my awareness have not intentionally deprived any living thing of life since I was born of the Ariyan birth. By this truth may there be well-being for you, and well-being for the conceived foetus".

The end of the Aṅgulimāla Sutta.

[10] BOJJHAṄGA SUTTA
The Discourse on the Seven Factors of Enlightenment

This sutta is the consolidated discourse on three similar events experienced by Reverend Mahā Kassapa, Rev. Moggallāna and Lord Buddha himself. These three were afflicted with disease, and were seriously ill and by the magical power of recitation of the *Bojjhaṅga Sutta*, each of them recovered from affliction and illness.

On one occasion, Lord Buddha was staying at Rājagaha, in the Bamboo grove, the feeding ground of black squirrels. At that time Rev. Mahā Kassapa was dwelling in the Pipphali Cave, afflicted with a disease and was seriously ill. The Lord visited him and expounded the doctrine of Seven Factors of Enlightenment. At the end of the preaching the Elder Kassapa recovered from affliction and illness disappeared. This is the first instance.

On another occasion, the Lord was staying in the same place at Rājagaha, in the Bamboo grove where the black squirrels were fed. Thereupon Rev. Mahā Moggallāna residing on the Gijjhakūṭa Hill, the Vultures' Peak, was afflicted with a disease and was gravely sick. So, the Lord visited him and preached the same doctrine of Seven Factors of Enlightenment to him. The Elder listened with due respect to him and recovered from that affliction. This is the second instance.

On the third occasion, while Lord Buddha was residing at the same town in the same Bamboo Grove, he himself was afflicted with a disease and suffered seriously. Then the Elder

Mahā Cunda approached the Lord, saluted him and attended him. The Lord requested the Elder Cunda to recite the Seven Factors of Enlightenment as usually expounded by the Lord Buddha and the Elder Cunda obeyed and recited.

"These Seven Factors of Enlightenment are lucidly expounded, are cultivated and are fully developed by the Blessed One. They are Mindfulness, Investigation of the Dhamma, Persevering effort, Rapture, Tranquility, Concentration, and Equanimity. These Seven Factors of Enlightenment conduce to perfect understanding, to full realization and to Nibbāna.

At the end, Lord Buddha approved the recitation. Then the Lord recovered from his affliction and thus his illness disappeared.

These three cases are put forth to indicate and to recommend the magical healing power of the recitation of the *parittas* and the Oath of Truth. Hence the Burmese medicine men practised and used to recite this *Bojjhaṅga Sutta* to help the patients recover quickly from their illness and to initiate successful medical treatments.

As a matter of fact, the original suttas are found expounded in prose form by Lord Buddha in *Mahāvagga Saṃyutta Pāḷi*. However, the ancient Burmese monks, who were expert in Pāḷi language composed the consolidated discourse into verse form to be known as the *Bojjhaṅga Paritta Sutta* of eleven stanzas.

Introduction

135) These seven dhammas are the factors of enlightenment, which eradicate all the suffering of the creatures who are transmigrating in the universal flux and which suppress the army of Death.

136) Having realized these seven dhammas, the creatures had attained the Immortality, the Fearlessness, Birthless – decayless and sickless stage; they became transcendental and liberated from three existences.

Oh thou! Let us recite this doctrine of Factors of Enlightenment;

137) Endowed with such and other qualifications altogether with innumerable qualities, this is a medicinal spell.

138) The factors of enlightenment are Mindfulness, Investigation of the Dhamma, Persevering effort, Rapture, Tranquility, and other factors of enlightenment.

139) The factor of Concentration and Equanimity. All these seven are well expounded by the All-seer, cultivated and amplified repeatedly by the Sage —

140) in order to discern profoundly, to realise the wisdom, and to attain Nibbāna;

By the asseveration of this truth, may you be happy forever.

141) At one time, the Lord saw Rev. Moggallāna and Rev. Kassapa suffering and sick, and he expounded the Seven Factors of Enlightenment.

142) The two Elders also were delighted there at and at that very moment were liberated from the sickness.

By the asseveration of this truth, may you be happy forever.

143) Once even the King of Dhamma, the Buddha himself was afflicted by sickness, then the Elder Cunda was requested to recite that very doctrine with due reference.

144) Having delighted, the Lord rose up thereupon from the sickness.

By the asseveration of this truth, may you be happy forever.

145) Just as the Defilements annihilated by Magga-consciousness, can arise again no more, in like manner these ailments were eradicated from the three Great Sages.

By the asseveration of this truth, may you be happy forever.

The end of the Bojjhaṅga Sutta.

[11] PUBBAṆHA SUTTA
The Discourse on Good Morning

This discourse of protection is so called *Pubbaṇha* — Good Morning, as the ancient wise sages had composed nineteen stanzas based on the three verses promulgated in the *Aṅguttara Nikāya — Pubbaṇha Sutta* and one verse in *Suttanipāta – Ratana Sutta.*

"Monks, whosoever beings at early morning, at noon, and at eve practise righteousness of body, speech and mind, such have a happy morning, a happy day, and a happy evening ..."

This *paritta* is necessarily recited for protection from epidemics, wars, and famine, especially from all calamities in conjunction with nine planets.

Though the name of the *paritta* is Good Morning, this is chanted at any time — in the morning, in the afternoon, or late in the evening. Being the eleventh *paritta* in this book of Discourse of Protection, we read the prayers and wishes, a sort of dissemination of Love or Lovingkindness to one's own self as well as to all other living creatures.

The announcement as "Oh thou! Let us recite" is absent here in this particular concluding sutta. This may be the reason that some scholars count only ten *Paritta Suttas* as authentic and justify that the Introductory part and this *Pubbaṇha Sutta* (concluding prayers) are later interpolations or rather non-canonical verses.

The entire *Paritta Suttas* are chanted, recited and sometimes spelled in terms of Apotropaic Religious fervour in

---

Gradual Sayings - Vol. I, p. 272.

Burma, expecting immediate results — or blessings — here and now, in this very life.

Introduction

146) The unlucky omen, the inauspicious event, and the unpleasant scream of evil birds, the undesirable dreadful planet, and miserable nightmare may all these be gone to disappear — by the glory of the Buddha.

147) The unlucky omen, the inauspicious event, and the unpleasant scream of evil birds, the undesirable dreadful planet, and the miserable nightmare, may all these be gone to disappear — by the glory of the Dhamma.

148) The unlucky omen, the inauspicious event, and the unpleasant scream of evil birds, the undesirable dreadful planet, and the miserable nightmare, may all these be gone to disappear — by the glory of the Saṅgha.

149) May all beings who are suffering be saved not to suffer.
May who are frightened be encouraged not to fear;
May who are in anxiety be cheered up not to be disappointed.

150) To such an extent we have accomplished the meritorious fulfilments.
May all the deities rejoice in this accomplishment.
In order to achieve all types of accomplishments,

151) may you give charity with full devoted faith;
may you observe the moral precepts constantly;
may you enjoy yourselves peacefully in meditation;
And all the deities who are present here may return to their respective abodes.

152) There is a certain strength of wisdom of all the Universal

Buddhas, all Individual Buddhas, and all *Arahants*, who had attained the Supreme Might. By the power of this strength, I fortify the protection all around me.

153) Whatever treasure there be either here or in the world beyond, whatever precious jewel here be in the heavenly abodes, there is no equality with the Tathāgata. This precious jewel is also in the Buddha. By this asseveration of the truth, may there be happiness to you.

154) Whatever treasure there be either here or in the world beyond, whatever precious jewel there be in the heavenly abodes, there is no equality with the Tathāgata. This precious jewel is also in the Dhamma. By this asseveration of the truth, may there be happiness to you.

155) Whatever treasure there be either here or in the world beyond, whatever precious jewel there be in the heavenly abodes, there is no equality with the Tathāgata. This precious jewel is also in the Saṅgha Order. By this asseveration of the truth, may there be happiness to you.

156) May all the auspices be with you! May all the deities protect you;

By the glorious power of all Buddhas, may you all be happy now and forever.

157) May all the auspices be with you; May all the deities protect you;

By the glorious power of all Dhammas, may you all be happy now and forever.

158) May all the auspices be with you; May all the deities protect you;

By the glorious power of all Saṅgha Orders, may you all be happy now and forever.

159) The most compassionate Lord had fulfilled all the required Perfections for the welfare of all beings, and had attained the Supreme Enlightenment.

By this asseveration of the Truth may you all be blissful now and forever.

160) Just as the Lord, the most affectionate of the Sakyas had triumphed through, at the foot of the Bo tree, so also may the victory be to you and may you be successful in all the auspicious conquests.

161) On the Unvanquishable Seat, above the summit of the most sacred earth being consecrated by all the Buddhas, the Lord had attained the Supreme Stage and rejoiced.

(In like manner may you rejoice too).

162) May good planets, good blessings, good dawn, good awakening, good moment, good instance, and offering good oblations to the Noble Sages, be to you.

163) May the physical act be sacred the verbal act be sacred, and the mental act be sacred. May you be established in these sacred things.

164) Having done the sacred acts, may you obtain the sacred gains; and having obtained the sacred issues, may you be happy and prosper in the Teachings of the Buddha.

May you, altogether with all your kinsmen be happy and be free from all types of disease.

The end of the Pubbaṇha Sutta.

Here ends the book of Eleven Mahā Paritta Suttas.

MAHĀ PARITTA PĀḶI
(Transliteration)

MAHĀ PARITTA PĀḶI

Namo tassa bhagavato arahato sammā sambuddhassa

Paritta-parikamma

1) Samanta cakkavāḷesu, atrāgacchantu devata,
saddhammaṃ Munirājassa ~ suṇantu saggamokkhadaṃ.

2) Dhammassavaṇakālo ayaṃ bhadantā.

3) Namo tassa bhagavato arahato sammā sambuddhassa.

4) Ye santā santacittā, tisaraṇasaraṇā, ettha lokantare vā,
bhummā bhummā ca devā, guṇagaṇagahaṇā, byāvaṭā sabbakālaṃ,
ete āyantu devā, varakanakamaye, Merurāje vasanto,
santo santosahetuṃ Munivaravacanaṃ sotumaggaṃ samaggaṃ.

5) Sabbesu cakkavāḷesu yakkhā devā ca brahmuno,
Yaṃ amhehi kataṃ puññaṃ sabbasampattisādhukaṃ

6) Sabbe taṃ anumoditvā samaggā sāsane ratā,
Pamādarahitā hontu ārakkhāsu visesato.

7) Sāsanassa ca lokassa vuḍḍhi bhavatu sabbadā,
Sāsanampi ca lokañca devā rakkhantu sabbadā.

8) Saddhiṃ hontu sukhī sabbe parivārehi attano,
Anīghā sumanā hontu, saha sabbehi ñātibhi.

9) Rājato vā, corato vā, manussato vā, amanussato vā,
aggito vā, udakato vā, pisācato vā, khāṇukato vā,
kaṇḍakato vā, nakkhattato vā, janapadarogato vā,
asaddhammato vā, asandiṭṭhito vā, asappurisato vā,
caṇḍa-hatthi-assa-miga-goṇa-kukkura-ahivicchika-
maṇisappa-

dīpi-accha-taraccha-sukara-mahisa-yakkha-
rakkhasādihi,
nānā bhayato vā, nānā rogato vā,
nānā upaddavato vā, ārakkhaṃ gaṇhantu.

Khuddakapāṭha 3–4.
Suttanipāta 318, 319.

MAṄGALA SUTTA

uyyojañña

10) Yaṃ maṅgalaṃ dvādasahi,
Cintayiṃsu sadevakā;
Sotthānaṃ nādhigacchanti,
Aṭṭhattiṃsañca maṅgalaṃ.

11) Desitaṃ Devadevena,
Sabbapāpavināsanaṃ;
sabbaloka hitatthāya,
maṅgalaṃ taṃ bhaṇāma he.

12) Evaṃ me sutaṃ:
ekaṃ samayaṃ Bhagavā Sāvatthiyaṃ viharati Jetavane Anāthapiṇḍikassa ārāme. Atha kho aññatarā devatā abhikkantāya rattiyā, abhikkantavaṇṇā kevalakappaṃ Jetavanaṃ obhāsetvā, yena Bhagavā tenupasaṅkami. upasaṅkamitvā Bhagavantaṃ abhivādetvā, ekamantaṃ aṭṭhāsi. Ekamantaṃ ṭhitā kho sā devatā Bhagavantaṃ gāthāya ajjhabhāsi:

13) "Bahū devā manussā ca maṅgalāni acintayuṃ
ākaṅkhamānā sotthānaṃ: brūhi maṅgalaṃ-uttamaṃ."

14) "Asevanā ca bālānaṃ, paṇḍitānañ-ca sevanā,
pūjā ca pūjanīyānaṃ: etaṃ maṅgalaṃ-uttamaṃ."

15) Paṭirūpadesavāso ca, pubbe ca katapuññatā,
attasammāpaṇidhi ca: etaṃ maṅgalaṃ-uttamaṃ.

16) Bāhusaccañ-ca sippañ-ca, vinayo ca susikkhito,
subhāsitā ca yā vācā: etaṃ maṅgalaṃ-uttamaṃ.

17) Mātāpitu-upaṭṭhānaṃ, puttadārassa saṅgaho,
anākulā ca kammantā: etaṃ maṅgalaṃ-uttamaṃ.

18) Dānañ-ca Dhammacariyā ca, ñātakānañ-ca saṅgaho,
anavajjāni kammāni: etaṃ maṅgalaṃ-uttamaṃ.

19) Ārati virati pāpā, majjapānā ca saññamo,
appamādo ca dhammesu: etaṃ maṅgalaṃ-uttamaṃ.

20) Gāravo ca nivāto ca, santuṭṭhī ca kataññutā,
kālena Dhammasavaṇaṃ: etaṃ maṅgalaṃ-uttamaṃ.

21) Khantī ca sovacassatā, samaṇānañ-ca dassanaṃ,
kālena Dhammasākacchā: etaṃ maṅgalaṃ-uttamaṃ.

22) Tapo ca brahmacariyañ-ca, ariyasaccānadassanaṃ,
nibbānasacchikiriyā ca: etaṃ maṅgalaṃ-uttamaṃ.

23) Phuṭṭhassa lokadhammehi, cittaṃ yassa na kampati,
asokaṃ virajaṃ khemaṃ: etaṃ maṅgalaṃ-uttamaṃ.

24) Etādisāni katvāna, sabbatthamaparājitā,
sabbattha sotthiṃ gacchanti: taṃ tesaṃ maṅgalaṃ-uttaman"-ti.

Maṅgala Suttaṃ Niṭṭhitaṃ

RATANA SUTTA

Uyyojañña

25) Paṇidhānato paṭṭhāya Tathāgatassa dasa pāramiyo, dasa upapāramiyo, dasa paramattha-pāramiyoti samatiṃsa paramiyo, pañca mahāpariccāge, lokatthacariyaṃ, ñātatthacariyaṃ, buddhatthacariyanti tisso cariyāyo, pacchimabhave gabbhavokkantiṃ, jatiṃ, abhinikkhamanaṃ, padhānacariyaṃ, bodhipallaṅke māravijayaṃ, sabbaññutaññaṇappaṭivedhaṃ, dhammacakkappavattanaṃ, nava lokuttaradhammeti sabbepime buddhaguṇe āvajjetvā Vesāliya tīsu pākārantaresu tiyāmarattiṃ parittaṃ karonto āyasmā Ānandatthero viya kāruññacittaṃ upaṭṭhapetvā:

26) Kotīsatasahassesu, cakkavāḷesu devata;
Yassānam pattigganhanti, yañca Vesāliyā pure,

27) Rogāmanussa-dubbhikkha sambhūtam tividham bhayam;
Khippa-mantaradhāpesi, parittam tam bhanāma he.

28) Yānīdha bhūtāni samāgatāni, Bhummāni vā yāni va antalikkhe,
Sabbeva bhūtā sumanā bhavantu, Athopi sakkacca suṇantu bhāsitam.

29) Tasmā hi bhūtā nisāmetha sabbe, mettaṃ karotha mānusiyā pajāya,
divā ca ratto ca haranti ye baliṃ, tasmā hi ne rakkhatha appamattā.

30) Yaṃ kiñci vittaṃ - idha vā huraṃ vā saggesu vā - yaṃ ratanaṃ paṇītaṃ

na no samaṃ atthi Tathāgatena, idampi Buddhe ratanaṃ paṇītaṃ,
etena saccena suvatthi hotu!

31) Khayaṃ virāgaṃ amataṃ paṇītaṃ, yad-ajjhagā Sakyamunī samāhito,
na tena dhammena samatthi kiñci, idampi Dhamme ratanaṃ paṇītaṃ,
etena saccena suvatthi hotu!

32) Yaṃ Buddhaseṭṭho parivaṇṇayī suciṃ, samādhim-ānantarikaññam-āhu,
samādhinā tena samo na vijjati, idampi Dhamme ratanaṃ paṇītaṃ,
etena saccena suvatthi hotu!

33) Ye puggalā aṭṭha sataṃ pasatthā, cattāri etāni yugāni honti,
te dakkhiṇeyyā Sugatassa sāvakā, etesu dinnāni mahapphalāni,
idampi Saṅghe ratanaṃ paṇītaṃ, etena saccena suvatthi hotu!

34) Ye suppayuttā manasā daḷhena, nikkāmino Gotamasāsanamhi,
te pattipattā amataṃ vigayha, laddhā mudhā nibbutiṃ bhuñjamānā,
idampi Saṅghe ratanaṃ paṇītaṃ, etena saccena suvatthi hotu!

35) Yathindakhīlo paṭhaviṃ sito siyā catubbhi vātehi asampakampiyo,
tathūpamaṃ sappurisaṃ vadāmi, yo ariyasaccāni avecca passati,
idampi Saṅghe ratanaṃ paṇītaṃ, etena saccena suvatthi hotu!

36) Ye ariyasaccāni vibhāvayanti, gambhīrapaññena sudesitāni,
kiñcāpi te honti bhusappamattā na te bhavaṃ aṭṭhamaṃ ādiyanti,
idampi Saṅghe ratanaṃ paṇītaṃ, etena saccena suvatthi hotu!

37) Sahāvassa dassanasampadāya tayassu dhammā jahitā bhavanti:
sakkāyadiṭṭhi vicikicchitañca, sīlabbataṃ vā pi yadatthi kiñci.

38) Catūhapāyehi ca vippamutto, chaccābhiṭhānāni abhabbo kātuṃ,
idampi Saṅghe ratanaṃ paṇītaṃ, etena saccena suvatthi hotu!

39) Kiñcāpi so kammaṃ karoti pāpakaṃ kāyena vācā uda cetasā vā,
abhabbo so tassa paṭicchādāya, abhabbatā diṭṭhapadassa vuttā,
idampi Saṅghe ratanaṃ paṇītaṃ, etena saccena suvatthi hotu!

40) Vanappagumbe yathā phussitagge gimhānamāse paṭhamasmiṃ gimhe,
tathūpamaṃ dhammavaraṃ adesayī, nibbānagāmiṃ paramaṃhitāya,
idampi Buddhe ratanaṃ paṇītaṃ, etena saccena suvatthi hotu!

41) Varo varaññū varado varāharo, anuttaro dhammavaraṃ adesayī.
idam-pi Buddhe ratanaṃ paṇītaṃ: etena saccena suvatthi hotu!

42) Khīṇaṃ purāṇaṃ navaṃ natthi sambhavaṃ,
virattacittā āyatike bhavasmiṃ, te khīṇabījā avirūḷhicchandā,
nibbanti dhīrā yathāyam-padīpo,
idam-pi Saṅghe ratanaṃ paṇītaṃ, etena saccena suvatthi hotu!

43) Yānīdha bhūtāni samāgatāni, bhummāni vā yāni va antalikkhe,
Tathāgataṃ devamanussapūjitaṃ, Buddhaṃ namassāma suvatthi hotu!

44) Yānīdha bhūtāni samāgatāni, bhummāni vā yāni va antalikkhe,
Tathāgataṃ devamanussapūjitaṃ, Dhammaṃ namassāma suvatthi hotu!

45) Yānīdha bhūtāni samāgatāni, bhummāni vā yāni va antalikkhe,
Tathāgataṃ devamanussapūjitaṃ, Saṅghaṃ namassāma suvatthi hotu!

Ratana Suttaṃ Niṭṭhitaṃ

Khuddakapāṭha 4–8.
Suttanipāta 312–315.

METTĀ SUTTA

Uyyojañña

46) Yassānubhāvato yakkhā, neva dassenti bhīsanaṃ;
Yamhi cevānuyuñjanto, Rattindivamatandito.

47) Sukhaṃ supati sutto ca, pāpaṃ kiñci na passati;
Evamādi guṇūpetaṃ, parittaṃ taṃ bhaṇāma he.

48) Karaṇīyam-atthakusalena, yanta santaṃ padaṃ abhisamecca;
Sakko ujū ca suhujū ca, suvaco cassa mudu anatimānī.

49) Santussako ca subharo ca, appakicco ca sallahukavutti;
Santindriyo ca nipako ca, appagabbho kulesvananugiddho.

50) Na ca khuddamācare kiñci, yena viññū pare upavadeyyuṃ;
Sukhino vā khemino hontu, sabbasattā bhavantu sukhitattā.

51) Ye keci pāṇabhūtatthi, tasā vā thāvarā va-navasesā;
Dīghā vā ye va mahantā, majjhimā rassakā aṇukathūlā.

52) Diṭṭhā vā ye va adiaṭṭhā, ye va dūre vasanti avidūre;
Bhūtā va sambhavesīva, sabbasattā bhavantu sukhitattā.

53) Na paro paraṃ nikubbetha, nātimaññetha katthaci na kañci;
Byārosanā paṭighasañña, nāññamaññassa dukkhamiccheyya.

54) Mātā yathā niyaṃ puttam, āyusā ekaputtamanurakkhe;
Evam pi sabbabhūtesu, mānasaṃ bhāvaye aparimāṇaṃ.

55) Mettañca sabbalokasmi, mānasaṃ bhāvaye aparimāṇaṃ;

Uddhaṃ adho ca tiriyañca, asambādhaṃ averam-asapattaṃ.

56) Tiṭṭhaṃ caraṃ nisinno va, sayāno yāvatāssa vitamiddho;
Etaṃ satiṃ adhiṭṭheyya, brahmametaṃ vihāra-midha māhu

57) Diṭṭhiñca anupaggamma, sīlavā dassanena sampanno;
Kāmesu vineyya gedhaṃ, na hi jātu ggabbhaseyya puna-reti.

Mettā Suttaṃ Niṭṭhaṃ

Khuddakapāṭha 10–11.
Suttanipāta 300–302.

KHANDHA SUTTA

Uyyojañña

58) Sabbāsīvisajātīnaṃ, dibbamantdgadhaṃ viya;
Yaṃ nāseti visaṃ ghoraṃ, sesañcāpi parissayaṃ.

59) Ānākkhettamhi sabbattha, sabbadā sabbapāṇinaṃ;
Sabbaso pi nivāreti, parittaṃ taṃ bhaṇāma he.

60) Virūpakkhehi me mettaṃ, mettaṃ Erāpathehi me;
Chabyāputtehi me mettaṃ, mettaṃ Kaṇhāgotamakehi ca.

61) Apādakehi me mettaṃ, mettaṃ dvipādakehi me;
Catuppadehi me mettaṃ, mettaṃ bahuppadehi me.

62) Mā maṃ apādako hiṃsi, mā maṃ hiṃsi dvipādako;
Mā maṃ catuppado hiṃsi, mā maṃ hiṃsi bahuppado.

63) Sabbe sattā sabbe pāṇā, sabbe bhūtā ca kevalā;
Sabbe bhadrāni passantu, mā kañci pāpamagamā.

64) Appamāṇo Buddho, appamāṇo Dhammo;
Appamāṇo Saṅgho, pamāṇavantāni sarīsapāni;
Ahi vicchikā satapadī, uṇṇanābhī sarabū mūsikā.

65) Katā me rakkhā, kataṃ me parittaṃ, paṭikkamantu bhūtāni;
Sohaṃ namo Bhagavato, namo sattannaṃ sammāsambuddhānaṃ.

Khandha Suttaṃ Niṭṭhaṃ

Vinaya Cūḷavagga 245.
Jātaka Vol. 1. 53–54.
Aṅguttara Vol. 1. 384.

MORA SUTTA

Uyyojañña

66) Pūrentam bodhisambhāre, nibbattaṃ morayoniyaṃ;
Yena saṃvihitārakkhaṃ, mahāsattaṃ vanecarā,

67) Cirassaṃ vāyamantāpi, neva sakkhiṃsu gaṇhituṃ;
"Brahmamantan" ti akkhātaṃ, parittaṃ taṃ bhaṇāma he.

68) Udetayaṃ cakkhumā ekarājā, harissavaṇṇo pathavippabhāso;
Taṃ taṃ namassāmi harissavaṇṇaṃ pathavippabhāsaṃ, tayājja guttāa vīharemu divasaṃ.

69) Ye brāhmaṇā vedagū sabbadhamme, te me namo, te ca maṃ pālayantu; Namatthu Buddhāmaṃ namatthu bodhiyā, namo vimuttānaṃ namo vimuttiyā; Imaṃ so parittaṃ katvā moro carati esanā.

70) Apetayaṃ cakkhumā ekarājā, harissavaṇṇo pathavippabhāso;
Taṃ taṃ namassāmi harissavaṇṇnaṃ pathavippabhāsaṃ;
Tayājja guttā viharemu rattim.

71) Ye Brāhmaṇā vedagū sabbadhamme, te me namo, te ca maṃ palayantu; Namatthu Buddhāmaṃ namatthu bodhiyā, namo vimuttānaṃ namo vimuttiyā. Imaṃ so parittaṃ katvā moro vāsamakappayi.

Mora Suttaṃ Niṭṭhitaṃ

Jātaka Vol. 1. 38–39.

VAṬṬA SUTTA

Uyyojañña

72) Pūrentaṃ bodhisambhare, nibbattaṃ vaṭṭajātiyaṃ;
Yassa tejena dāvaggi, Mahāsattaṃ vivajjayi.

73) Therassa Sāriputtassa, lokanāthena bhāsitaṃ;
Kappaṭṭhāyiṃ mahātejaṃ, parittaṃ taṃ bhaṇāma he.

74) Atthi loke sīlaguṇo, saccaṃ soceyyanuddayā;
tena saccena kāhāmi, saccakiriyaṃ-uttamaṃ.

75) Āvajjetvā dhammabalaṃ, saritvā pubbake jine;
Saccabalaṃ-avassāya, saccakiriyam-akāsahaṃ.

76) Santi pakkā apatanā, santi pādā avañcanā;
Mātāpitā ca nikkhantā, jātaveda paṭikkama.

77) Saha sacce kate mayhaṃ, mahāpajjalito sikhī;
Vajjesi soḷasa karīsāni, udakaṃ patvā yathā sikhī;
Saccena me samo natthi, esā me Saccapāramī.

Vaṭṭa Suttaṃ Niṭṭhitaṃ

Cariyāpiṭaka 415.
Jātaka Vol. 1. 9.

DHAJAGGA SUTTA

Uyyojañña

78) Yassā-nussaraṇenāpi, antalikkhe pi pāṇino;
Patiṭṭham-adhigacchanti, bhūmiyaṃ viya sabbathā,

79) Sabbupaddavajālamhā, yakkhacorādisambhavā;
Gaṇanā na ca muttānaṃ, parittaṃ taṃ bhaṇāma he

80) Evaṃ me sutaṃ —
Ekaṃ samayaṃ Bhagavā Sāvatthiyaṃ viharati Jetavane Anāthapiṇḍikassa ārāme.

81) Tatra kho Bhagavā bhikkhū āmantesi, "Bhikkhavo" ti,
"Bhaddante" ti te bhikkhū Bhagavato paccassosuṃ.
Bhagavā etadavoca:
"Bhūtapubbaṃ bhikkhave devāsura saṅgāmo samupabyūḷho ahosi.
Atha kho bhikkhave Sakko Devānamindo deve Tāvatiṃse āmantesi —
'Sace mārisā devānaṃ saṅgāma-gatānaṃ uppajjeyya bhayaṃ vā chambhitattaṃ vā lomahaṃso vā,
mameva tasmiṃ samaye dhajaggaṃ ullokeyyātha.
Mamaṃ hi vo dhajaggaṃ ullokayataṃ
yaṃ bhavissati bhayaṃ vā chambhitattaṃ vā lomahaṃso vā, so pahīyissati.

82) No ce me dhajaggaṃ ullokeyyātha,
atha Pajāpatissa devarājassa dhajaggaṃ ullokeyyātha.
Pajāpatissa hi vo devarājassa dhajaggaṃ ullokayataṃ,
yaṃ bhavissati bhayaṃ vā chambhitattaṃ vā, lomahaṃso vā, so pahīyissati.

83) No ce Pajāpatissa devarājassa dhajaggaṃ ullokeyyātha, atha Varuṇassa devarājassa dhajaggaṃ ullokeyyātha. Varuṇassa hi vo devarājassa dhajaggaṃ ullokayataṃ yaṃ bhavissati bhayaṃ vā chambhitattaṃ vā lomahaṃso vā, so pahīyissati.

84) No ce Varuṇassa devarājassa dhajaggaṃ ullokeyyātha, atha Īsānassa devarājassa dhajaggaṃ ullokeyyātha. Īsānassa hi vo devarājassa dhajaggaṃ ullokayataṃ yaṃ bhavissati bhayaṃ vā chambhitattaṃ vā lomahaṃso vā, so pahīyissatī ti.'"

85) Taṃ kho pana bhikkhave,
Sakkassa vā devānamindassa dhajaggaṃ ullokayataṃ,
Pajāpatissa vā devarājassa dhajaggaṃ ullokayataṃ,
Varuṇassa vā devarājassa dhajaggaṃ ullokayataṃ,
Īsānassa vā devarājassa dhajaggaṃ ullokayataṃ,
yaṃ bhavissati bhayaṃ vā chambhitattaṃ vā lomahaṃso vā,
so pahīyethāpi, nopi pahīyetha.

86) Taṃ kissa hetu?
Sakko hi bhikkhave, devānamindo avītarāgo avītadoso avītamoho,
bhīru chambhī uttarasī palāyīti.

87) Ahañca kho bhikkhave evaṃ vadāmi —
'Sace tumhākaṃ bhikkhave araññagatānaṃ vā rukkhamūlagatānaṃ vā
suññāgāragatānaṃ vā uppajjeyya bhayaṃ vā chambhitattaṃ vā lomahaṃso vā,
mameva tasmiṃ samaye anussareyyātha —

88) 'Iti pi so Bhagavā arahaṃ, sammāsambuddho, vijjācaraṇasampanno, sugato, lokavidū, anuttaro purisada-

mmasārathi, satthā devamanussānaṃ, buddho, bhagavā"ti.

89) Mamaṃ hi vo bhikkhave amussarataṃ
yaṃ bhavissati bhayaṃ vā chambhitattaṃ vā lomahaṃso vā, so pahīyissati.

90) No ce maṃ anussareyyātha,
atha Dhammaṃ anussareyyātha —

91) 'Svākkhāto Bhagavatā Dhammo,
sandiṭṭhiko, akāliko, ehipassiko, opaneyyiko,
paccattaṃ veditabbo viññūhī"ti

92) Dhammaṃ hi vo bhikkhave anussarataṃ
yaṃ bhavissati bhayaṃ vā chambhitattaṃ vā lomahaṃso vā so pahīyissati.

93) No ce Dhammaṃ anussareyyātha,
atha Saṃghaṃ anussareyyātha —

94) 'Suppatipanno Bhagavato sāvakasaṅgho,
ujuppaṭipanno Bhagavato sāvakasaṅgho,
ñāyappaṭipanno Bhagavato sāvakasaṅgho
sāmicippaṭipanno Bhagavato sāvakasaṅgho,
yadidaṃ cattāri purisayugāni aṭṭha purisapuggalā;
esa Bhagavato sāvakasaṅgho
āhuneyyo, pāhuneyyo, dakkhiṇeyyo, añjalikaraṇiyo,
anuttaraṃ puññakkhettaṃ lokassā"ti.

95) Saṅghaṃ hi vo bhikkhave anussarataṃ
yaṃ bhavissati bhayaṃ vā chambhitattaṃ vā lomahaṃso vā, so pahīyissati.

96) Taṃ kissa hetu?
Tathāgato hi bhikkhave arahaṃ sammāsambuddho vitarāgo vītadoso vītamoho, abhīru achambhī anutrāsī apalāyī ti.

97) Idamavoca Bhagavā,
idaṃ vatvāna Sugato; athāparaṃ etadavoca Satthā —

98) Araññe rukkhamūlevā, suññāgāre va bhikkhavo,
Anussaretha sambuddhaṃ, bhayaṃ tumhāka no siyā.

99) No ce Buddhaṃ sareyyātha, lokajeṭṭhaṃ narāsabhaṃ;
Atha Dhammaṃ sareyyātha, niyyānikaṃ sudesitaṃ.

100) No ce Dhammaṃ sareyyātha, niyyānikaṃ sudesitaṃ;
Atha Saṅghaṃ sareyyātha, puññakkhettaṃ anuttaraṃ.

101) Evaṃ Buddhaṃ sarantānaṃ, dhammaṃ saṅghaṃ ca bhikkhave;
Bhayaṃ vā chambhitattaṃ vā, Lomahaṃso na hessati.

Dhajagga Suttataṃ Niṭṭhitaṃ

Saṃyutta Nikāya Vol. 1. 220–222.

ĀṬĀNĀṬIYA SUTTA

Uyyojañña

102) Appasannehi Nāthassa, sāsane sādhusammate;
Amanussehi caṇḍehi, sadā kibbisakāribhi,

103) Parisānaṃ catassannaṃ ahiṃsāya ca guttiyā;
Yaṃ desesi Mahāvīro, parittaṃ taṃ bhaṇāma he.

104) Vipassissa ca namatthu, cakkhumantassa sirīmato;
Sikhissapi ca namatthu, sabbabhūtānukampino.

105) Vessabhussa ca namatthu, nhātakassa tapassino;
Namatthu Kakusandhassa, mārasenā-pamaddino.

106) Koṇāgamanassa namatthu, brāhmaṇassa vusīmato;
Kassapassa ca namatthu, vippamuttassa sabbadhi.

107) Aṅgīrasassa namatthu, sakyaputtassa sirīmato;
Yo imaṃ Dhammaṃ desesi, sabbadukkhāpanūdanaṃ.

108) Ye cāpi nibbutā loke, yathābhutaṃ vipassisuṃ;
Te janā apisuṇātha, mahantā vītasāradā.

109) Hitaṃ devamanussānaṃ, yaṃ namassanti Gotamaṃ;
Vijjācaraṇasampannaṃ, mahantaṃ vītasāradaṃ.

110) Ete caññe ca sambuddha, anekasatakoṭiyo;
Sabbe Buddhā samasamā, sabbe Buddha mahiddhikā.

111) Sabbe dasabalūpetā, vesārajjeh-upāgata;
Sabbe te paṭijānanti, āsabhaṃ ṭhānamuttamaṃ.

112) Sīhanādaṃ andante-te, parisāsu visāradā;
Brahmacakkaṃ pavattenti, loke appaṭivattiyaṃ.

113) Upetā Buddhadhammehi, aṭṭhārasahi nāyakā;
Battiṃsalakkhaṇūpetā, sītānubyañjanādharā.

114) Byāmappabhāya suppabhā, sabbe te munikuñjarā;
Buddhā sabbaññuno ete, sabbe khīṇāsava Jinā.

115) Mahāpabhā mahātejā, mahāpaññā mahabbalā;
Mahākāruṇikā dhīrā, sabbesānaṃ sukhāvahā.

116) Dīpā nāthā patiṭṭhā ca, tāṇā leṇā ca pāṇinaṃ;
Gatī bandhū mahessāsā, saraṇā ca hitesino.

117) Sadevakassa lokassa, sabbe ete parāyaṇā;
Tesā'haṃ sirasā pāde, vandāmi purisuttame.

118) Vacasā manasā ceva, vandām-ete Tathāgate;
Sayane āsane ṭhāne, gamane cāpi sabbadā.

119) Sadā sukhena rakkhantu, Buddhā santikarā tuvaṃ;
Tehi tvaṃ rakkhito santo, mutto sabbabhayehi ca.

120) Sabbarogā vinīmutto, sabbasantāpa vajjito;
Sabbaveram-atikkanto, nibbuto ca tuvaṃ bhava.

121) Tesaṃ saccena sīlena, khantimettābalena ca;
Tepi amhe-nurakkhantu, arogena sukhena ca.

122) Puratthimasmiṃ disābhāge, santi bhūtā mahiddhikā;
Tepi amhe-nurakkhantu, arogena sukhena ca

123) Dakkhiṇasmim disabhāge, santi devā mahiddhikā;
Tepi amhe-nurakkhantu, arogena sukhena ca.

124) Pacchimasmiṃ disābhāge, santi nāgā mahiddhikā;
Tepi amhe-nurakkhantu, arogena sukhena ca

125) Uttarasmim disābhāge, santi yakkhā mahiddhikā;
Tepi amhe-nurakkhantu, arogena sukhena ca.

126) Puratthimena Dhataraṭṭho, dakkhiṇena Virūḷhako;
Pacchimena Virūpakkho, kuvero uttaraṃ disaṃ.

127) Cattāro te mahārājā, lokapālā yasassino;
Tepi amhe-nurakkhantu, arogena sukhena ca.

128) Ākāsaṭṭhā ca bhūmaṭṭhā, devā nāgā mahiddhikā;
Tepi amhe-nurakkhantu, arogena sukhena ca

129) Iddhimanto ca ye devā, vasantā idha sāsane;
Tepi amhe-nurakkhantu, arogena sukhena ca.

130) Sabbhītiyo vivajjantu, soko rogo vinassatu;
Mā te bhavantarāyā, sukhī dīghayuko bhava.

131) Abhivādanasīlissa, niccaṃ vuḍḍhāpacāyino;
Cattāro dhammā vaddhanti, āyu vanno sukhaṃ balaṃ.

Ātānātiya Suttaṃ Niṭṭhitaṃ

Dīghanikāya. Pāthikavagga. 159.
Dhammapada, 29. 109.

AṄGULIMĀLA SUTTA

Uyyojañña

132) Parittaṃ yaṃ bhaṇantassa, nisinnaṭṭhānadhovanaṃ;
Udakampi vināseti, sabbameva parissayaṃ.

133) Sotthinā gabbhavuṭṭhānaṃ, yañca sādheti taṅkhaṇe;
Therassa Aṅgulimālassa, lokanāthena bhāsitaṃ;
Kappaṭṭhāyiṃ mahātejaṃ, parittaṃ taṃ bhaṇāme he.

134) Yato'haṃ bhagini ariyāya jātiyā jāto;
nābhijānāmi sañcicca pāṇaṃ jīvitā voropetā;
Tena saccena sotthi te hotu, sotthi gabbhassa.

Aṅgulimāla Suttaṃ Niṭṭhitaṃ

Majjhima Paṇṇāsa 306.

BOJJHAṄGA SUTTA

Uyyojañña

135) Saṃsāre saṃsarantānaṃ, Sabbadukkhavināsane, Satta dhamme ca Bojjhaṅge, Mārasenāpamaddane,

136) Bujjhitvā ye cime sattā, Tibhavā muttakuttamā, 1 Ajātimajarābyādhiṃ, Amataṃ nibbayaṃ gatā.

137) Evamādiguṇūpetaṃ, Anekaguṇasaṅgahaṃ, Osadhañ ca imaṃ mantaṃ, Bojjhaṅgañ ca bhaṇāma he.

138) Bojjhaṅgo satisaṅkhato, Dhammānaṃ vicayo tathā, Vīrimyaṃ pīti passaddhi, Bojjhaṅga ca tathāpare,

139) Samādhupekkhā bojjhaṅgā, Sattete Sabbadassinā Muninā sammadakkhātā Bhāvitā bahulīkatā.

140) Saṃvattanti abhiññāya, Nibbānāya ca bodhiyā, Etena saccavajjena, Sotthi te hotu sabbadā.

141) Ekasmiṃ samaye Nātho, Moggallānañ ca Kassapaṃ, Gilāne dukkhite disvā, Bojjhaṅge satta desayi.

142) Te ca taṃ abhinanditvā, Rogā mucciṃsu taṅkhane. Etena saccavajjena, Sotthi te hotu abbadā.

143) Ekadā Dhammarājā pi, Gelaññenābhipīḷito, Cundattherena taṃ yeva, Bhaṇapetvāna sādaraṃ.

144) Sammoditvāna ābādhā, Tamhā vuṭṭhāsi thānaso. Etena saccavajjena, Sotthi te hotu sabbadā.

145) Pahīna te ca ābādhā, Tiṇṇannam pi Mahesinaṃ, Maggahatā kilesāva, Pattānuppatti- dhammataṃ. Etena saccavajjena, Sotthi te hotu sabbadā.

Bojjhaṅga Suttaṃ Niṭṭhitaṃ

Saṃyutta Mahāvagga 71, 72, 73.

PUBBAṆHA SUTTA

Uyyojañña

146) Yaṃ dunnimittaṃ avamaṅgalañca, yo cā'manāpo sakuṇassa saddo;
Pāpaggaho dussupinaṃ akantaṃ, Buddhānubhāvena vināsam-entu.

147) Yaṃ dunnimittaṃ avamaṅgalañca, yo cā'manāpo sakuṇassa saddo;
Pāpaggaho dussupinaṃ akantaṃ, Dhammānubhāvena vināsam-entu

148) Yaṃ dunnimittaṃ avamaṅgalañca, yo cā'manāpo sakuṇassa saddo;
Pāpaggaho dussupinaṃ akantaṃ, Saṃghanubhāvena vināsam-entu.

149) Dukkhappattā ca niddukkhā, bhayappattā ca nibbayā;
Sokappattā ca nissokā, hontu sabbepi pāṇino.

150) Ettāvatā ca amhehi sambhataṃ, puññasampadaṃ;
Sabbe devā'numodantu, sabbasampattisiddhiyā.

151) Dānaṃ dadantu saddhāya, sīlaṃ rakkhantu sabbadā,
Bhāvanābhiratā hontu, gacchantu devatā' gatā.

152) Sabbe Buddhā balappattā, paccekānañca yaṃ balaṃ;
Arahantānañca tejena, rakkhaṃ bandhāmi sabbaso.

153) Yaṃ kiñci vittaṃ idha vā huraṃ vā, saggesu vā yaṃ ratanaṃ paṇītaṃ;
Na no samaṃ atthi Tathāgatena, idampi Buddhe ratanaṃ paṇītaṃ,
Etena saccena suvatthi hotu.

154) Yaṃ kiñci vittaṃ idha vā huraṃ vā, saggesu vā yaṃ ratanaṃ paṇītaṃ;
Na no samaṃ atthi Tathāgatena, idampi Dhamme ratanaṃ paṇītaṃ,
Etena saccena suvatthi hotu.

155) Yaṃ kiñci vittaṃ idha va huraṃ va, saggesu va yaṃ ratanaṃ paṇitaṃ;
Na no samaṃ atthi Tathāgatena, idampi Saṅghe ratanaṃ paṇitaṃ,
Etena saccena suvatthi hotu.

156) Bhavatu sabbamaṅgalaṃ, rakkhantu sabbadevatā;
Sabba-Buddhānubhāvena, sadā sukhī bhavantu te.

157) Bhavatu sabbamaṅgalaṃ, rakkhantu sabbadevatā;
Sabba-Dhammānubhāvena, sada sukhī bhavantu te.

158) Bhavatu sabbamaṅgalaṃ, rakkhantu sabbadevatā;
Sabba-Saṅghānubhāvena, sadā sukhī bhavantu te.

159) Mahākāruṇiko Natho, hitāya sabbapāṇinaṃ;
Pūretvā pāramī sabbā, patto sambodhimuttamaṃ,
Etena saccavajjena, sotthi te hotu sabbadā.

160) Jayanto bodhiyā mūle, sakyānaṃ nandivaḍḍhano;
Evameva jayo hotu, jayassu jayamaṅgale.

161) Aparājitapallaṅke, sīse puthuvipukkhale;
Abhiseke sabbaBuddhānaṃ, aggappatto pamodati.

162) Sunakkhattaṃ sumaṅgalaṃ, suppabhātaṃ suhuṭṭhitaṃ;
Sukhaṇo, sumuhutto ca, suyiṭṭhaṃ brahmacārisu.

Khuddakapāṭha, 5.
Suttanipāta, 312.
Aṅguttara Vol. 1. 299.

163) Padakkhiṇaṃ kāyakammaṃ, vācākammaṃ padakkhiṇaṃ;
Padakkhiṇaṃ manokammaṃ, paṇīdhi te padakkhiṇe.

164) Padakkhināni katvāna, labhantatthe padakkhine;
Te atthaladdhā sukhitā, virūḷhā Buddhasāsane;
Arogā sukhitā hotha, Saha sabbehi ñātibhi

Pubbaṇha Suttaṃ Niṭṭhitaṃ

Paritta Pāḷi Niṭṭhitā

MONASTIC SANCTION OF ACT OF BANISHMENT

Please listen unto me O Venerable Order of monks, these inhuman (*yakkha*) demons, (*ganddhabba*) musician-goblins (*kumbhanda*) devils, (*nāgā*) dragons and other evil spirits are cruel, ferocious, terrible, merciless and vexatious.

Their cruelty, ferocity, terror, mercilessness and vexation are seen and heard of (known).

If it is convenient to the Order (of monks), the Order may please perform the Act of Banishment to (upon) these inhuman demons, goblins, devils, dragons, and all other evil spirits from this house, and from this residential compound that these inhuman demons, goblins, devils, dragons, and all other evil spirits shall no more stay here in this house nor in this residential compound. This is the Announcement.

Listen unto me O Venerable Order (of monks) these inhuman demons, goblins, devils, dragons and other evil spirits are cruel, ferocious, terrible, merciless and vexatious.

Their cruelty, ferocity, terror, mercilessness and vexation are seen and heard of (known). The families annoyed by these spirits are also seen and heard of (known).

The Order performs the Act of Banishment to these inhuman demons, musician-goblins, devils, dragons, and other evil spirits from this house and from this residential compound; therefore, these inhuman demons, goblins, devils, dragons, and other evil spirits shall no more stay here in this house nor in this residential compound.

Therefore, this Act of Banishment is done to these inhuman demons, goblins, devils, dragons, and other evil spirits from this house and from this residential compound, in order that these inhuman demons, goblins, devils, dragons, and other evil spirits may no more stay in this house nor in this residential compound. If the long-lived Reverend One agrees, he may remain silent. If anyone does not agree, he may object articulately.

Secondly, I declare this meaningful statement.

Thirdly, I declare this meaningful statement.

The Order has (decreed) done the Act of Banishment to these inhuman demons, goblins, devils, dragons, and other evil spirits from this house and from this residential compound, so that they shall no more stay in this house nor in this residential compound. The Order yields consent and remains silent. Therefore, we understand that the Order agrees to this Act of Banishment.

PABBĀJANIYA KAMMAVĀCĀ

Namo tassa bhagavato arahato sammasambuddhassa

Suṇātu me bhante saṅgho, ime amanussā yakkha gandhabba kumbhaṇḍa nāgā caṇḍā rudhā rabhasā adayālukā vihesakā imesaṃ caṇḍatā ruddhatā rabhassaṃ adayālukatā vihesakatā dissanti ceva suyyantica. Kulānica imehi vihesitāni dissanticeva suyyantica. Yadi saṅghassa pattakallaṃ saṅgho imesaṃ amanussānaṃ yakkha gandhabba kumbhaṇḍanāgānaṃ imasmā gehā imasmā ārāmā pabbājaniya kammaṃ kareyya. Na imehi amanussehi yakkha gandhabba kumbhaṇḍa nāgehi imasmiṃ gehe imasmiṃ ārāme vatthabbanti. Esā ñatti.

Suṇātu me bhante saṅgho, ime amanussā yakkha gandhabba kumbhaṇḍa nāgā caṇḍā rudhā rabhasā adayālukā vihesakā imesaṃ caṇḍatā ruddhatā rabhassaṃ adayālukatā vihesakatā dissanti ceva suyyantica. Kulānica imehi vihesitāni dissanticeva suyyantica. Saṅgho imesaṃ amanussānaṃ yakkha gandhabba kumbhaṇḍa nāgānaṃ imasmā gehā imasmā ārāmā pabbājaniyakammaṃ karoti. Na imehi amanussehi Yakkha-gandhabba kumbhaṇḍa-nāgehi imasmiṃ gehe imasmiṃ ārāme vatthabbanti yassā-yasmato khamati imesaṃ amanussānaṃ Yakkha-gandhabba kumbhaṇḍa-nāgānaṃ imasmā gehā imasmā ārāmā pabbājaniya kammassa karaṇaṃ. Na imehi amanussehi yakkha gandhabba kumbhaṇḍa nāgehi imasmiṃ gehe imasmiṃ ārāme vatthabbanti, so tuṇhassa; yassa nakkhamati, so bhāseyya.

Dutiyampi etamatthaṃ vadāmi.

Tatiyampi etamatthaṃ vadāmi.

Kataṃ Saṅghena imesaṃ amanussānaṃ yakkha gandhabba kumbhaṇḍa nāgānaṃ imasmā gehā imasmā ārāmā pabbājaniya kammassa karoti. Na imehi amanussehi yakkha gandhabba kumbhaṇḍa nāgehi imasmiṃ gehe imasmiṃ ārāme vatthabbanti, khamati saṅghassa tasmā tuṇhi evemetaṃ dhārayāmīti.

Pabbājaniya Kammavācā Niṭṭhitā

ABOUT PARIYATTI

Pariyatti is dedicated to providing affordable access to authentic teachings of the Buddha about the Dhamma theory (*pariyatti*) and practice (*paṭipatti*) of Vipassana meditation. A 501(c)(3) nonprofit charitable organization since 2002, Pariyatti is sustained by contributions from individuals who appreciate and want to share the incalculable value of the Dhamma teachings. We invite you to visit www.pariyatti.org to learn about our programs, services, and ways to support publishing and other undertakings.

Pariyatti Publishing Imprints

Vipassana Research Publications (focus on Vipassana as taught by S.N. Goenka in the tradition of Sayagyi U Ba Khin)

BPS Pariyatti Editions (selected titles from the Buddhist Publication Society, copublished by Pariyatti)

MPA Pariyatti Editions (selected titles from the Myanmar Pitaka Association, copublished by Pariyatti)

Pariyatti Digital Editions (audio and video titles, including discourses)

Pariyatti Press (classic titles returned to print and inspirational writing by contemporary authors)

Pariyatti enriches the world by

- disseminating the words of the Buddha,
- providing sustenance for the seeker's journey,
- illuminating the meditator's path.

www.ingramcontent.com/pod-product-compliance
Lightning Source LLC
Chambersburg PA
CBHW071614040426
42452CB00008B/1341
9781681726908